Withdrawn

ISRAELI WOMEN

The Reality
Behind the Myths

LESLEY HAZLETON

SIMON AND SCHUSTER | NEW YORK

Copyright © 1977 by Lesley Hazleton
All rights reserved
including the right of reproduction
in whole or in part in any form
Published by Simon and Schuster
A Division of Gulf & Western Corporation
Simon & Schuster Building
Rockefeller Center
1230 Avenue of the Americas
New York, New York 10020
Manufactured in the United States of America
1 2 3 4 5 6 7 8 9 10

Library of Congress Cataloging in Publication Data

Hazleton, Lesley.
  Israeli women.

  Includes bibliographical references and index.
  1. Women—Israel. I. Title.
HQ1728.5.H39   301.41'2'095694   77-21587
ISBN 0-671-22531-6

Permission to reprint from the following is greatfully acknowledged:

  "Clockwork Doll," by Dalia Rabikovitz, Hebrew version © by Dalia
Rabikovitz, translation from Fourteen Israeli Poets, ed. Dennis Silk, Andre
Deutsch, 1977.
  "The Dove," by Dalia Rabikovitz, translation by Dom Moraes, re-

To No'a, aged ten, and her generation

Contents

Preface

Israel is a common first name among Israeli men. It was first used in the Bible when Jacob wrestled throughout the night with God and was given the name of Israel: "One who wrestles with God" (Genesis 32). The feminine form of the name is Israela. But Israela is rare among Israeli women, for women in the Jewish state do not wrestle with God.

This book is about Israela—the other, hidden Israel. Myths about Israeli women have attracted both the attention and the admiration of the world for over three decades. But the reality of their lives has remained well sheltered from the glare of publicity.

Not many noticed that Amos Elon's *The Israelis: Founders and Sons,* probably the best book on Israeli society, remains true to its title. It is a book about the male Israel; few women appear in its four hundred pages. And although there are only three women among the hundred and fifty personalities in the pages of the journalists Yuval Elizur and Eliahu Salpeter's *Who Rules Israel?,* one cannot accuse the authors of bias, since there is only a handful of women to choose from.

Where are Israeli women, then, if they have so little place at the forefront of their society? To answer this question, I have searched the shadows cast by the famous image of the liberated Israeli woman. My exploration led me to the main myths and ideologies by which the majority of Israeli women live. I have tried to shine some light on how these myths were

11

born and how they endure, and persist, as well as on the dynamics of the power they exert. This is, then, a preliminary sketch toward a social psychology of Israeli women.

Within Israel, the subject calls forth both controversy and defensiveness. For to examine the case of Israeli women is to look at the underside of Israeli society, the soft belly of its norms and values. And a different picture of Israel emerges.

As Western women have been moving slowly toward equality and a liberation from stereotyped sex roles, Israeli women have been shoring up the refuge of clearly "feminine" values and roles and rejecting feminism. Where femininity offers shelter, they realize, feminism offers struggle. Where femininity offers a quick and relatively easy road to economic and psychological security, feminism indicates a long and uncertain road. The difference is that femininity attains its end through a continuing dependence, and feminism by a break with that, by independence. And it is this difference that determines the quality of the security.

Given the harsh realities of Israeli life, the situation is understandable. In writing this book, therefore, I do not intend to convert. I barely hope to convince. My intention is to try to open a dialogue on women's status and roles in Israel, and to clear some of the dead tangle of ideology and mythology so that Israeli women can be seen, and can see themselves clearly.

Within such a dialogue, Israela may recognize her struggle. And out of that recognition she may find the strength to wrestle with her own image and emerge at the end of the night as Israeli in her own right.

L. H.
Jerusalem
April 1977

The 15 percent of Israeli women who are not Jewish but Arab, both Moslem and Christian, have been omitted from the scope of this book, since theirs is a unique situation. Their status is higher than that of most women in Arab countries, yet lower than that of Israeli Jewish women, a quandary complicated by the question of whether the majority identify themselves as Israeli or see their Israeli citizenship merely as a historical accident. Their language, their culture, their history and their faith are very different from those of the Jewish mainstream of Israeli society. I have confined myself to this mainstream, recognizing that, as a colleague once said, "When people abroad talk about Israelis, they mean Israeli Jews; when Israeli Jews talk about Israelis, they mean Israeli Jews; and when Israeli Arabs talk about Israelis... they mean Israeli Jews." Although I deplore this situation, it is the sad reality, and I have accordingly defined the scope of this book.

To ensure the privacy of the women quoted in this book by first name only, I have changed both the names and certain minor details of their lives. The pertinent facts, their feelings, their words, remain as they were told to me.

Thanks to my editor, Alice Mayhew, and to Joanna Ekman at Simon and Schuster for their help, advice and encouragement, to friends and colleagues in Jerusalem for their support, and to the hundreds of Israeli women with whom I talked and who remain anonymous in this book.

I

Three Myths

"The achievements of Israel's women have
become an axiom around the world."
—Beba Idelson,
first secretary-general of
the Working Women's Council[1]

"Our tragedy is that too many women are
pleased to be deprived of their rights."
—Member of Knesset
Shulamit Aloni[2]

The soft focus of old photographs gives them a lazy, dreamlike
quality. Beautiful young women, dark eyes shining, smile out
at us from sixty years ago. They have pitchforks slung over
their shoulders, and wear long cotton dresses and tough work
shoes. Standing in the middle of a cornfield, oxen and cart
beside them, they glow with health. A lamb under each arm,
their faces shine with contentment as they herd the sheep out
in the hills.

These are the *halutsot*, the women pioneers who left their
comfortable middle-class homes in Eastern Europe to follow
a vision of socialism, equality and justice in Palestine. By
1914 there were about two hundred of them, mostly spirited

seventeen-, eighteen- and nineteen-year-olds who took the socialist ideology of sexual equality at face value and expected
to find it by working on the soil in their new land.

Among them was Rachel Blaustein, later to become one
of the major Hebrew-language poets and a national poet of
modern Israel. She arrived in Palestine at age nineteen and
within the year was working in Kinnereth, an agricultural
settlement on the Sea of Galilee, hoping "to make music with
the hoe and to draw upon the earth." Such ideas were influenced by "Aleph Daled" Gordon, generally known simply as
"the Old Man," who had developed a new mysticism of labor
on the soil and the simple agricultural life. It was a natural
theme for a young woman just arrived from Russia and elated
by the Tolstoyan cult of the laborer. But Rachel Blaustein's
dream of agricultural bliss was to be rudely broken by the
First World War, which left her stranded on a French training
farm, and by illness.

Years later, in 1927, she wrote the swansong of her aspirations in what was to become one of her most popular poems:
"Perhaps." In many ways, the poem was to speak for her
fellow *halutsot*.

> And perhaps it was only a dream after all?
> And perhaps
> I never really went forth with the dawn
> to toil with the sweat of my brow?
>
> Can it be on those flaming and endless days
> when we reaped,
> that I never gave voice to a song as I rode
> on a cartful of sheaves high-heaped?
>
> That I never did bathe in the perfect and placid
> blue gleam
> of Kinnereth, my sea, ah Kinnereth, my own,
> were you real, then, or only a dream?[3]

For the majority of the *halutsot*, it was neither war nor
illness that shattered their dream, but the resistance of their

male "comrades" and the basic economics of earning enough food to live on. In the early years of Degania, a work group later to become the first kibbutz, women were not considered full-fledged members of the group. The men at Degania and at nearby Kinnereth were paid monthly wages by the Palestine Office of the Zionist movement. The women were not. They were not even listed in the annual contracts drawn up between the pioneers and the Palestine Office. When they insisted on being included, the women were told point-blank that they were working for the men and not for the Palestine Office.[4]

The tragedy was that this was true. For every new working group of twenty or so men breaking new soil and planting new fields, there were only three or four women, sometimes just one, and nearly all these women worked in the kitchen or the laundry. They found no music in the hoe and no earth to draw upon, only sixteen-hour days cleaning shirts and peeling vegetables. The men maintained that women in the fields would be an economic liability to the group, since their productivity was lower. A certain number could be taken in only to run the service side of affairs, no more.

But what of the proud philosophy of sexual equality? Surely that was an integral part of the new socialism? It was indeed—so integral a part, in fact, that it hardly needed to be, and therefore rarely was, spelled out. The outcome of avoiding explicitness was bitterly painful for the women.

"In Europe we planned and dreamed about our future in Zion; there, there was to be no distinction between men and women," wrote Sarah Malchin, one of the leaders of the early women settlers, in 1913. On reaching Palestine, however, "our beautiful dreams were destroyed by our hostile surroundings. . . . We girls were met with indifference and scorn everywhere."[5] Ridiculed by potential employers when they applied for agricultural work, the women then saw themselves abandoned by their male comrades. Although they had planned an egalitarian utopia together, the men now thought the women "absurd" for wishing to work alongside them.

The women had two options. The first was to identify

with the newfound motherland by claiming a mystic bond between woman's womb and the bowels of the earth, glorifying the mysterious workings of nature which only a female force could contact and understand—a biological mysticism which their granddaughters would develop in the Israel of the seventies. But snakebite, dysentery, typhoid, malaria and sheer hunger made this option ludicrous. There was no glory here, but a tough and arduous battle against a hostile land. The women were in far too difficult a conflict to indulge in the luxury of mysticism. The leap from the small-town Jewish shtetl or the warmth and comfort of more urbane and enlightened Jewish communities to the harshness of pioneering demanded a far greater psychological adjustment from the women than from the men, a more radical break of life-style and self-image. They had farther to fall in coming face to face with the disparity between their dream and its reality. So they chose a second option, incongruous but quick and simple: they tried to identify by dressing, behaving, talking and, wherever they could, working like men. Identification would open the way to automatic equality.

It was an idea that could only fail. A few stouthearted women started a special agricultural school to train women workers who would be an asset to any new kibbutz. They succeeded, though in terms of tens and not hundreds, until the school was shut down in 1921 by the British mandatory authorities "because of the climate." By then the ranks of women pioneers had grown from 6 percent to 17 percent of active socialist Zionists, and the male-dominated kibbutzim firmly refused to accept all of them as members. Some of the newcomers, desperate for work, joined the road-paving campaign run by the British authorities from 1920 to 1922, establishing a reputation as pavers of roads and hewers of rock. In fact, most of the three hundred women who worked the roads performed the same function as the women on the kibbutzim: they ran the kitchens and the laundries. In 1922 they were again out of work, and by 1925 the majority of working women in Palestine were unemployed. "Underemployment was usually their lot even when work abounded," wrote Ada Maimon, the historian of the women's movement in Palestine. "Inequality was the norm."[6]*

Young women exchanged their ideals for food, taking work as cooks and laundresses, seamstresses, office clerks and private maids—whatever work there was, wherever it was.

By the nineteen-twenties those women on kibbutzim were fighting a rearguard action. But Golda Meir, then a member of Kibbutz Merhavia, "couldn't for the life of me understand what all the fuss was about." The Merhavia women, she correctly observed, hated kitchen duty, not because it was hard, but because it was demeaning. These were young women who had no more idea how to cook than the men, and whose efforts were often met with derision. Meir saw their struggle "not as one for 'civic' rights, which they had in abundance [sic], but for equal burdens. They wanted to be given whatever work their male comrades were given—paving roads, building houses, or standing guard duty—not to be treated as though they were different and automatically relegated to the kitchen." It sounds reasonable enough, though Meir, eagerly feminine rather than feminist, stoutly declared that she "remained more concerned with the quality of our diet than with 'feminine emancipation.'"[7]

The Golda Meirs won the day. Meir's close friend and biographer Marie Syrkin sums up this transient epoch of feminism in her condescending preface to Ada Maimon's history of the movement: "Today the early feminist excesses of

---

* Some years later the women tried again. By 1930 there were six small training farms for women, which in due time served the additional purpose of immigrant absorption centers for single women, and eventually became general agricultural schools. Meanwhile the *halutsot* also had to struggle for basic political rights against the powerful religious sector of the Jewish community in Palestine at the time. By the late twenties it was clear that women could achieve even the most basic rights only by organizing separately, and from 1928 until 1948 it was the Working Women's Council that led the struggle for women's rights.

the *halutsa,* the woman pioneer, are a matter of the past.... The feminist concept of equality has become less literal and more rational."[8]

This "rationalism" helped transmute to myth another facet of the Israeli woman's image: the gun-toting fighter, ready to sacrifice her life for her country. Again there are the photographs from the past, this time from thirty or forty years ago. Now the women look tougher; dressed in fatigues, hair severely pulled back under caps, they train with full concentration and deadly seriousness. They are members of *Hagana,* the Jewish defense organization which fought the 1948 War of Independence and supplied the leadership and manpower for the Israel Defense Forces, formed right after the war.

The *Hagana* women knew how to use a gun. But it was generally the men who did the guard duty and the women who welcomed them home and, if necessary, nursed them. When things got too hot the women would clean and reload the rifles for the men, so that they could increase their rate of fire.

In the first stages of the War of Independence, in late 1947 and early 1948, women soldiers were essential for convoy duties, since they could conceal guns and grenades under their clothes and evade detection by the British troops manning the roadblocks, who did not search women. Some women served in the *Palmach,* the fighting arm of *Hagana,* as well as in the underground organizations of *Etzel* and *Lehi* (the Stern gang), but few were actually involved in combat once the war was under way. The winking condescension with which they were treated is expressed by Yigal Allon, at that time one of the leading *Palmach* commanders, in his history of the Israeli army: "The girls stormed at any proposed discrimination, arguing that it ran counter to the spirit of the new society being built in Palestine to restrict women to domestic chores, particularly since they had proven their competence as marksmen and sappers. In the end, the wiser counsel prevailed: the girls were still trained for combat, but placed in units of their own. Whenever possible, they were trained for defensive warfare only."[9] Allon's "wiser counsel" meant that women served as wireless operators, nurses, quartermasters—exactly as women served in the British army during World War Two. There were women who actually fought, and died, in battle, but it was solely on these exceptions that the rule of the myth was to be based.

Myths compel respect, not necessarily by their truth, but because they are needed by those who believe in them. It is not a rational need, certainly not a conscious need; but it is often vital, since myths lay the basis for a society's perception of itself, for its collective identity and the identity of every member of it. The myths touch, reveal and caress the core of any society's self-image.

The liberation of Israeli women is such a myth. For nearly three decades Israeli women have been the paradigm of women's liberation, the only example of feminism achieved in a world that has yet to awaken fully to the meaning of the word. They have made an essential contribution to Israel's self-image as good and progressive, the antithesis of its notoriously and cruelly sexist Arab neighbors. And the myth of their liberation has benefited Israeli women themselves, shoring up their self-esteem both as Israelis and as women.

It is an inspirational myth, and such myths die hard. They make good journalistic copy. They are exciting. They appeal to the idealist in all of us. Thus Western feminists have been no more immune to the power of the myth than others. The pride in Golda Meir, Israel's premier until 1974, was symptomatic. While nobody attempted to prove that Indian women were liberated by pointing to Indian Premier Indira Gandhi, "Look at Golda" became the slogan of the myth of Israeli women's liberation. The admiration Golda Meir inspired was largely an expression of the longing for women's liberation, a wishful perception of liberation achieved. In this sense, the myth of Israeli women's liberation is perhaps a creative myth, answering deep-rooted needs among women the world over.

But the destructive aspects of this myth far outweigh its creative potential for Israeli women. As the anonymous heroines of the myth, they have been assigned a symbolic existence. Their reality has been subordinated to the accepted image, and they have been relegated to the status of shadows, while the gap continues to widen between their public image and their real selves.

Today the multifaceted manifestations of the myth include the woman soldier just landed from a parachute jump or proudly marching, gun on shoulder, in parade; the tough kibbutz woman working the fields alongside the men or, pistol on hip, driving a tractor; the sexually uncomplicated urbanite who takes what she wants with no misgivings; and of course the tough, wizened politician taking her place in the arena of international politics. But only a few women soldiers are allowed to parachute, and then merely as a morale-booster. After basic training, army women rarely hold guns except on parade. One can count the number of Israeli women who drive tractors on the fingers of one hand. The urbanite uses her sexuality more for status than for pleasure. And the politician is an anti-feminist who shakes her head in amazement at the fact that no other Israeli woman has achieved a comparable level.

Faced with the facts, Israeli women are not fooled by the myth, but they appear to believe in it nevertheless. Open acknowledgment of disbelief would entail a potentially shattering reassessment of their status both as Israelis and as women, a painful shedding of their public image to bring their private pain into the open. Their attitude is one of suspended disbelief, making them willing victims of an empty but soothing ideology. Surrendering their real identity to the "cover identity" ascribed them by ideology, they move in a male world of reality in the false guise of equals.

The ideology of sexual equality was stated clearly in 1948 in Israel's Declaration of Independence: "The State of Israel will maintain equal social and political rights for all citizens, irrespective of religion, race or sex." It was reiterated in 1949, in the "basic guidelines" of the first government of Israel: "Complete and absolute equality of women will be upheld—equality in rights and duties, in the life of the country, society and economy, and throughout the entire legal system." Brave words, but empty ones, with neither the commitment nor the intention to carry them toward fulfillment. Neither statement had any legal binding. Both were purely declarative, and within two years both had been utterly compromised by the so-called Women's Equal Rights Law of 1951.

"A man and a woman shall have equal status with regard to any legal proceeding; any provision of law which discriminates, with regard to any legal proceeding, against women as women, shall be of no effect," states the first clause of this law. But three clauses farther down, the law revokes its own edict: "This law shall not affect any legal prohibition or permission relating to marriage or divorce," and "This law shall not derogate from any provision of law protecting women as women." Fully aware of what these clauses meant, the original proponent of the new law, Member of Knesset Rachel Kagan, abstained when it was voted through the Knesset. Within two years it was clear why. The Rabbinical Courts Jurisdiction (Marriage and Divorce) Law of 1953 awarded the religious establishment monopolistic control over marriage and divorce for all Jewish citizens, thus legalizing the sexism of Orthodox Judaism. And one year later, the Employment of Women Law forbade women to work at night on the grounds that this is injurious to their health.

Few bothered to read beyond the titles of such laws, and devotees of the myth could thus remain oblivious to what could qualify as a large-scale political confidence trick. For genuine sexual equality was never a goal of the new state.

The myth of achieved equality was to take the place of real achievement. It resolved the conflict between ideology and emotion by denying the existence of conflict—a defense mechanism of flight rather than fight, which required false constructs to shore it up. For despite an intellectual commitment ot women's liberation, the emotional commitment was to the traditional role of women.

By 1948 Israel had been through four decades of experimentation and socialism, fighting and pioneering. Now that the state was founded, it wanted, above all, normalization—

and normalization included normal sex roles. The lip service
paid to ideology solved problems of conscience by banishing
them from public awareness. The everyday contradictions that
inevitably arose between ideology and reality were met with
the attitude, "We already have laws for sexual equality—if it
does not exist in practice, then it is because women are not
really interested in it."

The institutionalization of socialist Zionism within the
confines of the new state meant the putting aside of ideology
in favor of pragmatism. The "Robin Hood role" that political
sociologist David Apter ascribes to prestatehood nationalism[10]
was both compromised and bureaucratized—and Maid Marian
remained where she had been all along, in the forest.

It is a familiar forest. The statistical account of women's
involvement in Israel's public life is dismal. There are no
women in the cabinet, no women director-generals of government ministries, no women mayors. There are only eight
women among the 120 members of the Knesset (parliament).
In both academe and government service, women's repre-
sentation is pyramidal, with many women at the bottom
of the ladder and few or none at the top. Women are 48
percent of first-degree university students; by doctoral level,
they receive 13 percent of the degrees; and they are a mere
2 percent of full professors. Women make up 39 percent of all
civil servants in Israel but only 9 percent in the higher grades.[11]

Women are 1 percent of the country's engineers, 7 percent of its jurists and—the one exception to Western countries
—25 percent of its doctors, mainly pediatricians and family
doctors. Aside from medicine, women comprise less than 10
percent of professional and managerial personnel. They are
12 percent of Israel's journalists, the vast majority of them
snugly tucked into women's pages and magazines. Only 6
percent of working women, as opposed to 24 percent of men,
are employers or self-employed.

No more than 51 percent of eighteen-year-old girls are
called to serve their "compulsory" two years in the Israel
Defense Forces. There are no women generals in the I.D.F.;
the highest rank held by a woman is colonel.

Little more than one third of Israel's women work out-side their homes (compared with 46 percent in the U.S., for example). Their average annual income is 60 percent of men's, and their average hourly wage about 75 percent that of men.[12] The lower the work status, the greater the difference between male and female wages. The most striking statistic, in a country that has boasted an Equal Pay for Women Law since 1964, is that women working alongside men in plants and offices throughout Israel, doing the same work, may get an hourly wage anywhere from 25 to 40 percent less than that of the men beside them on the assembly line or in the office.

"An employer will pay the same wages to a working woman as he would pay to a man at the same place of work for the same work or for work which is essentially equal," the law says. The two sectors that adhere strictly to the law are academe and the civil service, but the rarity of women at the top in these sectors places in question their commitment to the spirit and not just the letter of the law. Elsewhere, covert discrimination is regularly practiced. Different work titles for men and for women in effect contravene the law, but it is almost impossible to prove that work is "essentially equal." The nationwide federation of labor unions, the Histadrut, quietly sanctions such practices, and has even obstructed attempts to bring cases to court. The law has no authority.

New legislation is easier to create than a change in people's ingrained modes of thinking and relating to others. Attitudes care nothing for legislators' agenda, nor for legal print. Although sexual equality in this instance has the power of the law behind it, that power is meaningless without authority. True authority resides in public assent to the power of the law, and without that assent, the law is reduced to two possibilities: enforcement against the will of the population (which smacks too much of totalitarianism for any country calling itself a democracy), or quiet inefficacy.

Legal change without psychological change alters the surface picture; illusions of progress are created, and legislators can congratulate themselves in the conviction that by pronouncing the problem cured they have actually cured it.

At best, however, the psychological situation remains the same. At worst, the laws become counterproductive. By contributing to the myth of sexual equality in Israel, they aggravate the real problem of inequality.

The combination of factors here is unique: an ideology in which few really believed, but which was essential to the self-esteem of the many; a history which glorifies the struggle to realize that ideology, seen through the admiringly telescopic eyes of a later generation that chooses to concentrate on a minority phenomenon; laws which purport to uphold the ideology but which, in phrasing or application, are purposely ineffectual; and a myth which makes true practice of the ideology all but impossible. The myth and the ideology exist in symbiotic union. While the ideology reinforces the myth by giving it rational justification, the myth rationalizes the ideology by assuming it fulfilled. It would be the perfect self-perpetuating system were it not that it takes no account of the reality of experience. Experience—that of the *halutsot* and the women fighters of history, and that of Israeli women today—is negated.

This negation of experience indicates the failure of the ideology. One of ideology's main functions, as the psychologist Erik Erikson expressed it, is "the tendency at a given time to make facts amenable to ideas, and ideas to facts, in order to create a world image convincing enough to support the collective and individual sense of identity."[13] In Israel, the ideology of sexual equality worked perfectly for the collective, the State of Israel, giving it a strong identity as progressive and egalitarian. But it undermined the identity of the individual, the Israeli woman, by placing her experience in complete contradiction to the ideals to which her country subscribed. This clash between ideals and reality, expectations and possibilities, is touchingly expressed by one kibbutz woman, Yael, from Horshim in the coastal plain: "What in fact do the feminists want from us? Do they want to create frustration between aspirations and the reality of possibilities on the kibbutz? Equal rights means equal opportunities, but to push girls toward unrealistic aspirations and expectations will only increase the rate of their leaving the kibbutz."[14] In this sense, the whole of Israel is the kibbutz.

The contradiction between ideology and reality is too great to tolerate consciously; the velvet curtain of ideology hides too harsh a reality. The contrast must be muted so that women can accept it intellectually without feeling that they have merely resigned themselves to it, and so that they can maintain their self-respect as people without forfeiting their self-respect as women.

What women needed was the comfort of an identity that would place the gap between ideology and reality in a happier light.

That comfort came offering all the ease and relief of a large, well-padded, old-fashioned armchair after a hard day's work. It was so "obvious" and "natural" a solution to the search for identity that it required just a sigh of relief from struggle, a small step backward, and Israeli women, aided by their government, could relax into a soothing counter-mythology to the mythology of equality. This was the biological myth, the antidote to the myth of liberation.

The basic assumption of the biological myth is that women are defined, both physically and psychologically, by their biology. This counters the myth of liberation in three major areas. First, it offers an alternative basis for self-esteem by positing that women's child-bearing capacity is of overriding importance, the major factor in any woman's life and therefore a prime determinant of her personality, abilities and desires. It presents reproduction as women's incomparable and unique contribution as citizens of their state, and as their prime channel for fulfillment as human beings. All else, in comparison, is unimportant. Second, the biological myth justifies inequality as protection. It says that women should not be forced into legal equality lest their biological and psychological vulnerability make their situation harder than, instead of equal to, that of men. Equality is an ideal, but reality demands that women be protected. And third, the biological myth supplies women with a refuge from the struggles and responsibilities of adult life. They are closed in the home, unaware of the main political and social issues which shape their lives. It is the women who create life; but it is the men who shape it.

Theodor Herzl, "the spiritual father of the Jewish state," as he is called in the Declaration of Independence, etched the pattern of liberation overridden by biology in his utopian novel *Altneuland (Old-New Land)*, written in 1902 and perhaps more accurately prophetic in its description of women's role than on any other point. In Herzl's scheme of things, women in Israel would work until they marry, and then become full-time wives and mothers. In a discussion with the narrator, Kingscourt, the politician hero describes his wife: "She nursed our little boy, and so forgot a bit about her inalienable rights. She used to belong to the radical opposition. That is how I met her, as an opponent. Now she opposes me only at home, as loyally as you can imagine, however." Says Kingscourt, "That's a damned good way of overcoming the opposition. It simplifies politics tremendously." The politician smugly replies, "I must make it clear to you, gentlemen, that our women are too sensible to let public affairs interfere with their personal well-being."[15]

Though Israeli women today do not regard their situation as utopian, they certainly agree that it is sensible. This is how things are; therefore this is how they are naturally meant to be; therefore this is how they ought to remain. For women, the question of equality with men does not arise, for women have different aims in life, different modes of thinking and feeling, and different concepts of what is important. The difference in bodies determines the difference in minds . . . and the difference in legal status.

Hebrew University sociologist Rivka Bar-Yosef, the only top-flight Israeli academic concerned with thorough investigation of the reality of Israeli women's lives, characterizes the Israeli legal view of women as "dissimilar but equal." While paying lip service to the ideology of equality, the law in fact protects the biologically and socially prescribed feminine roles. The legal logic is the tortuous one of the inequality of equality. "These 'ascriptive' laws have a protective tendency," writes Bar-Yosef, "their rationale being the assumption that, due to biological attributes, women are more vulnerable than men. Hence, formal equality based on assumptions of complete similarity results in discrimination."[16] The result is a cynical concept of equality, and a highly paternalistic view of women's place in society.

The 1954 Employment of Women Law limits employment of women at night on the grounds of possible damage to their health. The Defense Service Act of 1959 specifies a shorter period of compulsory military service for women than for men and different kinds of training and employment in service, and it specifically exempts from any form or period of service all women who are married, pregnant or have children. Under the National Insurance Act of 1953, women retire at age sixty and men at age sixty-five, the official explanation being that women still function as homemakers and therefore should not be burdened with a double role beyond the age of sixty. Thus the primacy of women's role as wives and housewives is implicitly sanctioned by law, and the tax authorities concur by refusing to consider a working woman's expenses in payment of other working women (a cleaning woman or a child nurse) as tax-deductible.

None of these laws encourage women to take a full and equal part in Israel's public life. Many women feel that they have little choice in the matter. The paucity of day nurseries,* the short primary school day ending at noon, lower pay and slimmer chances of promotion discourage women from taking a work role seriously. Due to one bright star in the Employment of Women Law, which states that an employer may not fire a pregnant woman and that she is allowed up to three months' paid leave of absence after giving birth (which is covered by National Insurance), employers tend to avoid placing women in positions of responsibility, arguing that women may get pregnant and then disappear from work for

---

* The 500 or so day nurseries currently in operation serve less than half the population of working mothers of infants and young children.

three months. The fact that nearly every Israeli working man serves anywhere from thirty to eighty days of reserve military service each year, with his salary also covered by National Insurance, does not occur to them as a reason not to employ men.

It is too much to fight against in a country which has plenty of wars already. So Israeli women tend to work from the time they leave school or graduate from the army until their marriage or first pregnancy, and then drop out. Women are nearly half the work force in the fourteen-to-twenty-four age group (the ratio is high owing to the large number of young women who do not serve in the army and instead work in low-paid jobs until marriage); in the twenty-five to thirty-four age range women make up less than a third of the work force; by forty-five to fifty-four they are a quarter; and by fifty-five and over they are scarcely more than one fifth.[17] There is no "reentry" phenomenon in Israel as there is in the United States, since forty-year-old women who have spent the last twenty years in the home prefer the role of grandmother to almost certain rejection in the labor market.

Those women who work do so almost entirely out of economic necessity.[18] What with one of the highest tax rates in the world, booming inflation, and the race to achieve a decent standard of living in a country still wavering precariously between pre- and post-industrialism, an extra income is vital for many families. If a woman does not work, it is a kind of status symbol, a sign to the world that her husband can support his family without his wife's help. The wealthier of such wives may engage in volunteer activities, raising funds for charities, but most of their time is spent around the pool, at the hairdresser's, dressing up to stroll through the shops or linger in a café with friends. These are either the elite, the top of the bunch in the almost entirely Ashkenazi* establish-

---

* Ashkenazi Jews are those of Western origin, generally East European. The early Zionists were almost exclusively Ashkenazi—and from founding the State it was an easy step to almost total control of the political establishment of Israel today. While they were the

ment that runs Israel, or the nouveaux riches, wives of busi-
nessmen who made it big in the economic boom following the
Six Day War of 1967.

Paradoxically, the other major group of nonworking wives
is at the very bottom of the social scale, women from traditional Oriental backgrounds, whose husbands will not tolerate
their working outside the home. These are the two extremes of
Israeli women: the rich with time on their hands and luxury,
and the poor whose lives are a timeless grind of drudgery.
And yet both act as showcases of their husbands' ability. The
former reflect his professional or social status, the latter his
virility in having as many children as possible and his pride
and honor in not having to live on a woman's earnings.

The big difference is that the poor work like slaves. Although they are accounted too weak to drive trucks or tanks
by the army, and too vulnerable to work night shifts by the
government, they lug up to thirty kilos of food at a time from
the markets, scrub down tile floors and beat out rugs by hand,
wash the dishes and the diapers in iron basins, sometimes
without hot water, and spend all of Thursday and Friday
preparing food for the Sabbath. Vacuum cleaners, dishwashers,
electric mixers and washing machines, even ovens, are generally unknown commodities to these women. Their life is
back-breaking, physically tough and mentally exhausting.
Says psychologist Shoshana Sharni, who has spent years working with illiterate mothers of large families, all of Moroccan
or Yemenite origin: "These women lead monotonous lives
and are continually tired, not only physically but mentally,
an exhaustion of resignation."[19] Their main burden is ex-

---

overwhelming majority of Palestinian Jews in 1948, Ashkenazi
are now 45 percent of Israel's population. The majority, the
Sephardi Jews (the name derives from the Hebrew for Spanish but
applies to all Oriental Jews whose families came from North Africa
or the Middle East), are generally socially, politically and economically inferior, despite their numerical superiority, and are sometimes referred to as "the second Israel"—the Israel behind the
successful appearances of the Ashkenazi establishment.

tremely low self-esteem, with no faith in their ability to change their situation.

Between the extremes of wealth and poverty, the gap between Ashkenazi and Sephardi Israeli women is still great. Whereas the former marry at an average age of twenty-two and their average number of children is 2.8, the latter marry earlier, at twenty, and their average number of children is 4.6. Some 95 percent of Ashkenazi women have had formal schooling, over a third for more than eight years, and more than half now work outside the home. Only 56 percent of Sephardi women have attended school, less than a third of them for more than eight years, and only 20 percent work outside the home.[20]

But these statistics tell only part of the story, since they include the whole range of Israeli women: mothers and daughters, pioneers, refugees and native-born citizens. What they cannot show is that the daughters are narrowing the gap—in attitude if not yet in concrete achievement—between Sephardi and Ashkenazi. As the Sephardi daughters reach adulthood, for example, their main aim in life, constantly reiterated, is "not to be like my mother." None of the drudgery, none of the burden of many children, none of the waiting on husband as lord and master. These young women are determined to build another kind of life for themselves, and their role model is drawn from the largely Ashkenazi middle class. Thus while the Ashkenazi women have thoroughly feminized the suffragette image over the past three decades, the Sephardi women are trying to move forward into the same modern version of traditionalism. The two groups are reaching toward a consensus on what it is to be a woman, searching for a concept of modern femininity in which biological differences are protected rather than abused or ignored, and being a woman becomes a virtue in itself.

The Ashkenazi role model takes liberation for granted, so much so that there is no need to act on it. "Of course Israeli women are liberated," says Adina, an attractive blonde of twenty-five who, until she married, was a nurse. "It's all there in the laws. If it doesn't show up in your statistics, then

it's simply because we don't choose to avail ourselves of it.
Look at me, of course I could go on nursing, but I prefer to
stay at home and be a good mother instead of trying to do
everything all at once. Why on earth should I want to make
life hard for myself?"

"Of course all those things that the *halutsot* did are possible," says Devorah, twenty-nine, who works in the children's
house of one of Israel's largest and richest kibbutzim. "But
what woman in her right mind would want to do all that?
Getting dirty, breaking your back in the fields, sweating under
a hot sun, getting old before your time—no thanks, not for
me. A woman's role is to take good care of herself so that she
can be at her best for her husband and her children."

"Of course a woman should have outside interests, be
involved in her society, know what's going on and be able to
take an intelligent interest in it," says Ruth, forty-two, loung-
ing among the enveloping cushions of her Danish sofa, with
the curtains half-closed against the glare of the late-morning
Tel Aviv sun. "But let's face it, a woman's real interest in life
is in two things—children and love—and these are what she'll
seek for her satisfaction above all else."

"Of course." The theoretical value of the myth of liberation is accepted, but it is the biological myth that governs
women's lives. Israeli women use biology as a "masking
myth,"[21] a popular ideology which serves to cover and relieve
contradictions in the official picture of liberation. But it is
inadequate to its task, and only creates further strain as the
dissonance between the two worlds of self-image, liberated and
biological, sharpens into a potential double bind of schizo-
phrenogenic proportions.* An element of choice must be in-
troduced to avert this danger, and it is this element that
Israeli women rely on in creating the third of the three

---

* The "double bind" theory of schizophrenia[22] poses the following
conditions: *a.* two mutually exclusive sets of expectations, presented
simultaneously but on different levels of communication; *b.* no way
out. A situation, in other words, of "damned if you do, damned if
you don't."

main myths which shape their lives: the myth of the "real woman," based not on the vulnerability of femininity as is the biological myth, but concentrating on its privileges.

This development of biology into blessing arises from resignation but transcends it by creating the impression of choice. Choice is a basic assumption of the liberated myth; it does not exist in the biological one. Those women who believe in the liberated myth but live the biological one—the elite and the increasingly affluent middle class in Israel—feel it important to demonstrate that they have chosen, thus retaining at least the illusion of liberation. And yet they see no way to overcome what is known in the kibbutz movement as "the biological tragedy of the woman." The tragedy is therefore raised to the highest level, where instead of being pitied for their femininity, women are to be protected, valued, admired and envied by men. The "real woman" myth places them on a quasi-mystic pedestal to which men can never attain. It emphasizes sexual differences in an attempt to make a virtue out of femininity, to create a positive self-image that would only be demeaned by any suggestion of being put on a level with men. An elusive and closed world of femininity is created. And it would be crazy, given these assumptions, to choose anything other than to be a "real woman."

Betty Friedan's depiction of the feminine mystique accurately portrays the philosophy of this "real woman." "The feminine mystique says that the highest value and the only commitment for women is the fulfillment of their own femininity. It says that the great mistake of Western culture, throughout most of its history, has been the underevaluation of this femininity. It says this femininity is so mysterious and intuitive and close to the creation and origin of life that man-made science may never be able to understand it. . . . The mistake, says the mystique, the root of women's troubles in the past, is that women envied men, women tried to be like men, instead of accepting their own nature, which can find fulfillment only in sexual passivity, male domination, and nurturing maternal love."[23]

In the first two decades of the State of Israel, the realities of life were too harsh for women to swathe themselves in such silk-and-satin wrappings of femininity. But since 1967, when the standard of living began to rise, a growing Israeli middle class has discovered the virtues and vices of a minor but slowly increasing degree of affluence. And as the material quality of their lives has improved, Israeli women have gravitated toward this more affluent version of the biological myth, romanticizing and intellectualizing it to the level of an art.

The real-woman myth offers an aura of feminine self-fulfillment that flatters and glorifies its subject. "Anything I write about real women must read oddly, except perhaps to real women themselves, or the occasional man whom some accident of birth or experience tempts to agree with me," wrote Robert Graves in the sixties,[24] extending an esoteric invitation to a hidden, secret reality, available only to those with the insight and sensitivity to probe beneath the coarse shell of appearances. It is a dangerous little secret. It glorifies the pain of women's lives, praising them for being "real women" despite all the burdens they have to bear. It gives them an insidious pat on the shoulder, together with the time-worn line, "Man's biological function is to do, woman's is to be."

In Israel, where the men defend their country in war after war and the women are the protected, such a philosophy finds easy acceptance. It was tragically and poignantly expressed after the 1973 Yom Kippur War by Naomi Zorea, a member of Kibbutz Maagan Michael, whose second son had died in that war, her first having died in the Six Day War in 1967. In an open "Letter to the Daughters of Israel" she expressed the woman's role in Israel at war. "No, ours is not an impotent participation in the process of human history," she exclaimed. "We bestow things that are as basic as sun and soil. We bestow life itself, and the first pleasures, food, feel, smell, the beginnings of the capacity to love. . . ." Sitting with other women in mourning, she recalled, ". . . we were five sad, strong women sitting there. It was so sad, yet it was such a marvelous experience. Suddenly I felt as though the five of us sitting there were five mothers out of antiquity, out of mythology, whose power causes them to turn into goddesses." The mothers are the strong, the determiners of fate, not the determined. "If a nation is worthy," Zorea concluded, "its mothers are Graces. If not, they are Destroyers. And the borderline between the two is thin, very thin."[25]

This is part of the role of the "real woman" in Israel, the woman who makes what Premier Yitzhak Rabin, in a speech for International Women's Year, called "the supreme sacrifice"—not her own death, but that of her husband or son.[26] It is a role she carries with the "inborn dignity" that Robert Graves notes as distinguishing real women, but it is also one that can create enormous stress.

With the web of femininity spun tight around her, the Israeli woman is in danger of retreating into a self-spun cocoon, living a rich fantasy life which has nothing to do with the eminently practical accommodations which another part of her is willing to make with her everyday world. Graves' glorification of the feminine mystique and his presentation of women as lost earth-mothers from a previous age, merely acting out their part in modern society, describes a very real phenomenon now growing among Israeli women: the withdrawal from a contradictory reality into a comforting fantasy, not to such an extent as to hinder everyday functioning, but enough to give the woman a personal faith in the meaning of her own existence.

"A real woman somehow avoids suicide or virtual suicide or the mental institution, but is always painfully aware of having been born out of her true epoch," writes Graves.[27] This attitude surfaces sometimes in small signs of a longing for romanticism, harkening to a bygone age of chivalry, so simple and tempting when seen in the misted retrospect of a few hundred years. For instance, fighter pilots, the epitome of Israeli virility, are sometimes called "medieval knights," since they generally fight in close combat, one-to-one. And the paratroopers, nearly as high as the pilots in the Israeli woman's esteem, were referred to as "our noble stallions" during the Six Day War. A 1976 edition of *Ha-Shavua,* the magazine of the once-radical Kibbutz Artzi organization, illustrated an article on the difficulties of kibbutz women with the romantic drawings of Aubrey Beardsley—flowingly robed ladies gazing longingly at languid knights, and, on the cover, long-tressed women peering down from the turrets of a medieval tower as their knights return from the wars.

This is the new direction of Israeli women's fantasies: not equality, nor motherhood, but a deep yearning for the protected yet vulnerable times of yore, when men indeed "did" and women indeed "were."

And what of the legend of liberation? Dalia Rabikovitz, Israel's leading woman poet, limns its demise in her poem "The Dove," written appropriately in medieval ballad style:

> There was once a white dove, once on a day.
> Ah, love this dove—
> She sprouted a wing and flew away.
> Ah, love this dove.
>
> On the way she met the Raven King.
> Ah, love this dove—
> She met on the way a wolf-pack howling.
> Ah, love this dove.
>
> She saw seventy-seven enemies.
> Ah, love this dove—
> Birds struck at her and had jealous eyes.
> Ah, love this dove.
>
> She was white till the day she was devoured.
> Ah, love this dove—
> From her whiteness and wing a legend flowered.
> Ah, love this dove.[28]

2

The Judaic Yoke

"Blessed art Thou O Lord our God, King of
the Universe, that Thou hast not made me a
woman."
—from the daily prayers
of Orthodox Judaism

Israeli Jews are Israeli by citizenship, but Jewish by nationality. It is this legal anomaly that makes religion a central issue
in Israeli life and catapulted Anne Shalit, a publicity-shy Scots-
born biologist, to the status of a cause célèbre in Israel in
1968. A non-Jew and an atheist whose grandfather was an
ardent advocate of the Jewish state, she had married Benjamin
Shalit, a tall, burly naval psychologist who was writing a doctoral thesis on behavior under stress. The Shalits were to
undergo three years of stress as they waged a frontal assault
in the courts on one of the fundamental principles of the
Jewish state: the definition of who is a Jew.

It had been tacitly accepted that anyone who declared
himself a Jew was one. But the Shalits challenged the hitherto
unbreakable link between religion and nationality in Israeli
law when they went to register the birth of their two sons.
They declared that the children were of no religion, but
nevertheless demanded that the boys be registered under *le'om*

(nationality) as Jewish. The children were clearly not Jewish under *halacha,* the rabbinical law, since their mother was not Jewish. But both parents declared themselves atheists and claimed that their children were Jewish by cultural affiliation, though not by religion. It was an important distinction. As non-Jews, the boys would be unable to marry Jews in Israel, where there is no civil marriage, and might well be subject to a flow of small discriminations on the part of the Ministry of the Interior, controlled by the main political party of Israel's religious establishment—the National Religious Party.

The Shalit case came to a tense climax in January 1970, when nine Supreme Court judges split five to four in favor of the Shalits and against the Ministry of the Interior. The Shalits, flushed with victory, threw a boisterous party. "Relax," Benjamin told me exultantly, "this country is well on the way to becoming one of the most secular countries in the world." From the man who was soon to become chief psychologist of the Israel Defense Forces, it was a remarkable piece of wishful thinking.

Within weeks of the Supreme Court judgment, the Shalit case led to a coalition crisis that nearly brought down the government, dependent as it was on the National Religious Party to keep the coalition in power. Reconciliation came in the wake of an amendment to the Law of Return, which guarantees automatic Israeli citizenship to all Jews arriving in Israel; henceforth a Jew was legally defined as one born to a Jewish mother or converted to Judaism—the religious definition demanded by the National Religious Party. When the Shalits attempted to register a third child, three years later, all loopholes were closed; the Orthodox Jewish establishment was more deeply entrenched than before. Anne Shalit's third child is thus a non-Jew, and the Shalits are now living in Sweden.

Far from being one of the most secular countries in the world, Israel defines and constantly redefines itself in terms of its religion. In 1948 the Declaration of Independence specifically stated that Israel was to be a Jewish state. And so it is. For while it is Israel the nation that provides the norms and modes of everyday existence, it is Judaism that gives meaning to life as an Israeli. In recognition of this fact, as much as in obedience to the realities of power politics, the State of Israel has given full legal sanction to the power of the Jewish religion over its citizens' private lives.

Israel is not just a Jewish state; it is also a Judaic one. The Orthodox Judaic definition of Jewishness is the only clear-cut one available. And the political power of the religious establishment is a concrete assertion of Jewishness in a state whose raison d'être stems from the Jewish experience in the past. The Jewish religion provides the most tangible expression of a deeply felt but vague sense of Jewish peoplehood, of a shared fund of occasional joy and abundant tragedy and sorrow.

The partnership of synagogue and state began in the nineteen-thirties, when the secular Jewish administration in Palestine gave in to the pressures of the religious Zionist organizations for the sake of a united Zionist front. But the full force of the "theopolitic"[1] was not felt until 1953, when the Rabbinical Courts Jurisdiction (Marriage and Divorce) Law came into effect. This law, passed by the new State of Israel, gave the religious establishment full control in matters of personal status—a precedent established by the British Mandate, but which many had hoped the new State of Israel would change.

The law states: "Matters of marriage and divorce of Jews in Israel, being nationals or residents of the State, shall be under the exclusive jurisdiction of the Rabbinical courts. Marriages and divorces of Jews shall be performed in Israel in accordance with Jewish religious law." The theopolitical establishment administers both secular and religious laws, making mincemeat of Israel's much-vaunted legislation on the equality of women.

By giving secular legal status to religious law, Israel has raised an insuperable barrier to equality for women. To call the laws of Orthodox Judaism (the only Judaism accepted in Israel) sexist is an understatement: they do not recognize woman's existence as a full human being. To say that they promote a double standard avoids the issue: they promote only one standard, the male one.

Women are not allowed to give evidence in Rabbinical courts, the courts that control marriage and divorce, since they are considered emotionally unreliable. As the Talmud says: "Women are temperamentally light-headed."[2] Women are classed together with children, the mentally deficient, the insane and criminals, none of whom can testify in Rabbinical courts. Women cannot be judges in these courts either. They have no place in the public life of Judaism, whose attitude to women in public is succinctly expressed by Joseph Caro, author of the fifteenth-century code of Jewish law, the *Shulhan Aruch*:[3] "A man shall not walk between two women, two dogs or two pigs, and two men shall not allow a woman, a dog or a pig to walk between them."

Orthodox Jewish law on marriage and divorce, as it applies to all Jewish Israeli citizens regardless of whether they are religious, is based on two fundamental principles: first, that the woman is the property of her husband, and second, stemming from the first, that polygamy is permissible.

The Jewish marriage ceremony specifically states that the woman is the "sanctified property" of her husband. As such, she is forbidden to all other men. Thus, while a wife may not have sexual relations with anyone other than her husband, her husband is a free spirit—except with regard to someone else's wife. Then he transgresses, not sexual morality, but the property right of another man, and is therefore punishable alongside the woman. In biblical times both were stoned to death; today the woman can still be pressured to divorce against her will for having an extramarital affair. Moreover, once divorced she is allowed neither to marry her lover nor to remarry her husband. She is declared *asura le'baala u-le'boala*, forbidden to husband and lover, in a superbly Old Testament act of revenge. And the Rabbinate, since it controls marriage, enforces this ordinance.

The woman remains the man's property until he consents to a divorce or until he dies. Thus a woman whose husband has disappeared and is presumed dead—a real possibility in

Israel, where husbands have disappeared in the Nazi Holocaust or have been killed, mangled or burned beyond identification in later wars—is designated *aguna,* anchored. She is anchored to the spirit of a husband who is most probably, but not beyond any shadow of doubt, dead. If she remarried while there was still any doubt she would risk the invalidation of that marriage should her first husband be alive, in which case she would be an adulterous woman, forbidden to both first and second husbands. Rather than face this possibility, she is forbidden to remarry. If she dares the ban, knowingly or unknowingly, her children and their descendants for ten generations will suffer. They will be declared *mamzerim,* the only form of bastardy in Judaism. Bastardy in the Judaic view is the result not of unknown paternity, but of illegal paternity, where one man has infringed another's property rights by attempting to beget children on property not his. Thus a child born of an adulterous (or incestuous) relationship is a *mamzer,* a kind of demi-Jew forbidden to marry any other Jews except converts and other bastards. This ban is handed down to the child's descendants for ten generations, by which time the taint of adultery has presumably been weakened and they are allowed back into "the community of Israel."

These laws stem from the concerns of a Bronze Age tribe wandering the Middle East, eager to define itself apart from the other tribes of the region by ensuring genetic homogeneity, and strongly concerned with matters of property rights and inheritance. At that time, such a code defined women's status with clarity, and assured women the protection of a husband. In the twentieth century, however, they are barbaric.

The most famous bastardy case in Israel was that of the Langers, a brother and sister who discovered, when they both wanted to marry in 1971, that they were bastards under Jewish law, and forbidden to marry their intended partners. It was a long, complicated story. Their mother, Eve, had married a Christian in Poland before World War Two. After their marriage, he converted to Judaism, undergoing circumcision, to appease her parents. The couple separated in Palestine in 1942, and a local rabbi assured Eve that since her husband's conversion was not valid under *halacha,* she needed no divorce. She married again in 1944, becoming Eve Langer. Her second husband died in 1952. When she attempted to marry for a third time in 1955, she found herself forbidden to do so because the Rabbinical court held that her first husband's conversion was indeed valid, that she was therefore still married to him, that she could not remarry without divorcing him— and that her marriage with Langer had been adulterous. Without informing her, the court had branded her children by Langer bastards. Since the Langer son was in the army, he appealed to then Defense Minister Moshe Dayan for help. A two-year public scandal ensued. This was resolved by Shlomo Goren, formerly chief chaplain of the Israel Defense Forces and newly elected as one of Israel's two chief rabbis, who declared Eve Langer's first marriage null and void, since her first husband's conversion was not up to the standards of *halacha.* Thus the siblings married, and the stigma was transferred to the first husband—this time not the stigma of bastardy, but of being a non-Jew.

Two other escapes from the maze of halachic legislation, one private and one very public, demonstrate the absurdity of these laws in modern Israel. In the first case, thirty-two-year-old Ronit had been married for eleven years, and she and her husband, Avi, were constant fixtures in Tel Aviv's bohemian-artistic circle. Then Avi left Ronit and their two children to go and live with another woman, with whom he subsequently had a child. Ronit asked for a divorce. His answer: certainly, if it is financially worth my while . . . "Here is this completely irreligious so-called bohemian," said Ronit, eyes wide in exasperation, "using the medieval precepts of the *halacha* and the religious laws of this country, which he's always scoffed at, to extort money from me that I don't have and wouldn't give him if I did. What incredible hypocrisy!" Ronit was nearly trapped, for she had no hope of a divorce unless Avi granted her one. Under Jewish law, the man must first agree to grant the divorce paper, then the woman has to assent to accept it—an ideal arrangement when both sides are in agreement, and an impossible one when there is bitterness, often leading to blackmail of this type. Moreover, Ronit could not do what Avi did—simply live with her lover and, if she wanted, have a child with him—for she would be severely penalized for it. While Avi's new child is quite legitimate—since the woman he lives with is not married—any child that Ronit had with someone else would be designated a bastard. Moreover, she would be forbidden ever to marry her lover should she finally get a divorce.

Fortunately Avi left one point out of his reckoning. The two had been married in a civil ceremony outside Israel, and the Rabbinical courts are not averse to annulling such marriages. Although the courts cannot openly force anyone to grant or accept a divorce, they can, in cases such as this, declare Ronit and Avi's marriage null and void, since it was not in accordance with *halacha*. Since Avi clearly has another family, and polygamous situations are not so easily accepted now as thirty years ago, Ronit may yet find herself, if not divorced, at least free to marry as a single woman.

Status is the open secret of the second story. When former Defense Minister Moshe Dayan married his second wife, Rachel Koren, in June 1973, the ceremony was performed by the chief chaplain of the Israel Defense Forces, despite the fact that the marriage was in flagrant contradiction of halachic law. It was common knowledge in Israel that the couple had been lovers since the early sixties, and that when their affair started Rachel was still married. Although she soon obtained a divorce, the date of the start of the affair, never a point of contention, should have meant that Rachel was *asura le'baala u-le'boala*—forbidden to marry Dayan.[4] But Dayan, by virtue of his popular political status, could safely and openly flout the religious law that is binding on less highly placed individuals.

Rachel Koren and Ronit both tangled with the rabbinical law because a woman may not have a lover, though a man may. In principle, Judaism is polygamic, and though the *herem derabenu gershom* (the sixteenth-century ban of Rabbi Gershom on most forms of polygamy) held for European Jews, Oriental Jews regularly practiced polygamy until they arrived

in Israel, where it is forbidden—under civil law. Under religious law, which overrides civil law in such cases, it is permissible. Thus, while a rabbi is forbidden to sanctify a
polygamous marriage on pain of imprisonment, any such marriage once performed is valid. In some cases, as when the wife
is declared "rebellious,"* or when she is in a mental hospital
or is barren, the Rabbinate can sanction polygamous marriage,
and the polygamy is then legal under civil law too.

Polygamy lies behind another strange throwback to ancient times practiced in Israel today by law: the Levirate Law,
which states that a childless widow must marry her husband's
brother, even if he is already married, so that he can fulfill his
dead brother's duty of being fruitful and multiplying, thus
ensuring that his brother's name will not die out. While a
child of such a union is acknowledged as the living brother's
seed, it carries the dead brother's name. The wife's role in this
instance is clear: her function is to ensure her husband's
posterity.

This law is based on the famous scene in Genesis 38,
where Tamar's husband dies, leaving her childless. Her father-
in-law, Judah, orders Onan, his second son, to "Go in to thy
brother's wife, and perform the duty of a brother-in-law to
her, and raise up offspring for thy brother." This order was
not to Onan's taste. He "knew that the offspring would not
be his," and therefore, as the saying goes, he "threshed within
and spilt without." For this crime Onan was killed by God's
wrath: for depriving his dead brother of progeny, through
coitus interruptus, and not, as popular belief has it, for
masturbation.

By the time it was codified in Deuteronomy as the Levirate Law, Onan's legacy incorporated an "out"—the ceremony
of *halitsa,* in which the widow shows her disgust and contempt
at the brother's refusal to marry her by taking off his shoe

---

* A rebellious wife, called a *moredet,* is one who leaves her husband
against his will. A wife who flees a husband because he beats her
can thus be declared a *moredet* and divorced against her will without child custody.

and spitting on him, saying, "Thus shall be done to that man who will not build up his brother's house." Nowadays *halitsa* is usually preferred to Levirate marriage. But no childless widow can remarry without going through the ceremony, since otherwise she is considered betrothed to her brother-in-law. Ada, a twenty-five-year-old graphic artist whose husband died of cancer, says that she found the ceremony "disgusting and degrading. Now I'm free to remarry, but I'll leave it awhile —I've had enough of the Rabbinate for now."

Ada was lucky. Her brother-in-law made no problems about *halitsa*. But many young widows are subjected to blackmail: the brother-in-law may simply refuse to participate in the ceremony until the widow pays him a certain sum of money. The widow thus has the unpleasant option of paying or remaining bound to her brother-in-law and unable to marry. In Israel, where many young husbands have been killed in the wars before having children, such blackmail is a well-known phenomenon, and one against which the widow has no legal recourse.

A strange and insidious romanticization of Levirate Law formed the plot of the Israeli film *I Love You, Rosa,* written and directed by Moshe Mizrachi in 1973. Set in the Old City of Jerusalem at the turn of the century, the film follows the story of Rosa, a beautiful twenty-one-year-old childless widow, and Nissim, her eleven-year-old brother-in-law. Since Nissim is not allowed to give *halitsa* until age eighteen, Rosa is bound to him until then. "Life is laughing at both of us," she tells him as the two suffer through an unfulfilled sexual relationship when she takes him into her house after he runs away from home. The film ends with the couple eventually falling in love and marrying. There is no spitting, no blackmail, no suffering—just the sun setting into the Judean Hills as the film fades to a close.

A host of further restrictions on who may marry whom emphasizes the Judaic concern with genetic purity. Marriage between a Jew and a non-Jew, for example, is impossible in Israel. Such a couple would have to travel abroad to marry, and their children could marry Jews in Israel only if the mother is Jewish. The same dilemma sometimes faces couples when one of the partners has converted by any other means than the halachic ritual of Orthodox Judaism. (Reform and Progressive conversions are not recognized, though they are often allowed to slip by, especially since the influx of Russian immigrants from the U.S.S.R. in the last few years has brought a considerable number of couples in which one partner went through a "quickie conversion" in Vienna in order to enter Israel as a citizen under the Law of Return.) Any man with a sexual injury or defect is forbidden to marry, since he will not be able to fulfill his duty of having children. A descendant of the Cohen caste (the high priests in the days of the Temple) cannot marry a divorcee, a widow, or a prostitute, since he may be called on to officiate at the new Temple, if and when it be built, and must retain his purity by having to do only with virgins. A notable case in this connection was that of Supreme Court Justice Haim Cohen, who went to the United States to marry his wife, a divorcee, in open contempt of the Rabbinical laws. Cohen was strongly attacked for his marriage on his return to Israel, and there were many demands for his resignation; but he held fast to both position and principle and is considered legally married, since a "forbidden marriage" that is not incestuous or adulterous is binding once performed. (Cohen is one of the five judges who ruled in favor of separation of nationality and religion in the Shalit case.)

Not all members of the Cohen caste, however, have the surname Cohen. Those who do, or who have surnames traditionally belonging to the caste (such as Katz or Kaplan), have no way out except marriage abroad, with all the expense involved. But those who do not can simply deny that they are Cohens in order to marry whom they wish. It is thus a common ploy to lie like a trooper in the Rabbinical courts for love's sake, since by so doing couples avoid being branded *psul hitun*—unmarriageable. Former marriages abroad are simply not mentioned; divorcees have suddenly met their second husbands just a couple of months previously, when in fact they had been lovers long before her divorce; and, until the amendment to the Law of Return after the Shalit case, immigrants would simply declare themselves Jewish at the Ministry of the Interior, whatever their religion. Journalist Yoela Har-Shefy, who has extensively investigated the handling of "unmarriageables," sums up the situation tartly: "Whoever among them doesn't know how to lie, pays dearly."

Marganit Levy of Beer-Sheba found out just how dearly. When her divorce came through at the end of 1973, Levy asked the Rabbinical court to send the divorce certificate as quickly as possible, explaining that she was pregnant by her lover, with whom she had been living for the two years she was separated but not yet divorced from her husband, and that she wanted to marry him before the child was born. The court obliged and sent the certificate posthaste—with the phrase *asura le'baala u-le'boala,* forbidden to husband and lover, stamped across it. Appealing her case to the Supreme Court, Levy won Israel's first secular divorce certificate on a technicality: under a new order to the Rabbinical courts, the forbidding rider should have been placed on a separate certificate and not on the divorce certificate itself. But Levy still cannot marry her lover and the father of her child, since the civil court cannot marry them and the Rabbinical court refuses to do so. Like the Shalits, she won a pyrrhic victory.

Close tabs are kept on citizens such as Levy. In September 1975 a short-lived scandal broke when 144 computerized blacklists kept by the Ministry of Religious Affairs and distributed to the Rabbinical courts were leaked to the press. The very existence of the lists had been kept a closely guarded secret by the Ministry of the Interior, the Ministry of Religious Affairs and the Rabbinical courts. Some of them included bastards and suspected bastards, divorced women and their lovers, and Jews converted by other than strictly halachic means or with names and backgrounds that made their Jewishness doubtful. All were branded unmarriageable. Journalist Har-Shefy, who was sheltered by nuns as a girl in Nazi-controlled Poland and passed as an Italian Catholic, observed bitterly, "My mother's name was Christina, but that didn't prevent her being sent to Treblinka concentration camp. It would have prevented her being accepted as a Jew in Israel, though."

The blacklists are still kept. The director-general of the Ministry of Religious Affairs told me at the time that his ministry had "no intention of stopping the lists." And indeed there is no legal apparatus to stop them. The Rabbinical courts continue to impose archaic precepts on twentieth-century women, and remain unmoved by the disgust of a large portion of the general public and even of some Orthodox religious figures. Rabbi Menahem Hacohen, for example, a Labor Party Member of Knesset known as "the Histadrut rabbi" for his long-standing connection with the trade union federation, calls the Rabbinical courts "a Kafkaesque nightmare." "What goes on in these courts," he says, "is a dialogue between the deaf that usually ends in the woman's oppression and discrimination against her."5

One of the most amazing items of Orthodox Jewish legislation, and one little known since instances of it are rare, is the *isha katlanit,* the fatal woman. This is a woman who has been widowed three times, all three husbands dying of natural causes. The three deaths are laid at the feet of the woman, who is then declared quite literally fatal and forbidden to marry again. This law expresses a basic discrepancy in the Jewish attitude toward women: while the woman is the means to continuity, both of her husband and of the Jewish people, she also threatens it.

The law of the fatal woman is a logical outcome of the attitudes that created the laws of *niddah* (impurity). Based on Leviticus 18:19 ("You shall not approach a woman to uncover her nakedness while she is in her menstrual uncleanness"), these laws are disgusting in their disgust of women; they are truly pornographic. *Niddah* is fortunately not part of the civil code of Israeli law, since it cannot be enforced, but it reveals the Judaic attitude toward women's bodies—an attitude of fear and revulsion.

Codified in perverse detail by Joseph Caro in the *Shulhan Aruch,* the laws of *niddah* forbid sexual intercourse not only during menstruation but for at least seven days after, to ensure that the woman is perfectly "clean." Defiance of this law supposedly can lead to premature death for both part-

ners.[6] The detailed means of avoiding this danger make hor-
rifyingly fascinating reading. "To touch her [a menstruating
woman] in a caressing manner is punishable with lashes,"
wrote Caro. "He is not permitted to come into contact with
her, even with his little finger; he should not hand anything
over to her, be it even a long thing, nor should he receive
aught from her; he is likewise forbidden to throw anything
from his hand into her hand, neither is she permitted to throw
aught from her hand into his hand." The two cannot sleep
together. He must not sit where she sat. But since he has to
eat and drink and his wife has to provide for these needs, she
is permitted to prepare food and drink for him as long as
she does not do so in his presence. She must then set the food
on the table when he is out of the room; if he is in the room
and sees her doing so, he cannot touch the food.

More details follow in abundance, delving into the exact
color and quantity of any "moisture oozing out of her body."
A woman with a vaginal discharge due to a fungal infection is
apparently pure, while just the suspicion that she has started
menstruating, even if there is no blood, is enough to make her
impure.

This impurity lasts a minimum of twelve days. During
the seven days after menstruation, the woman must examine
herself carefully each day: "Examinations, whether at the end
of her menstruation or during the seven clean days, must be
made with an old white linen cloth or with a soft white
woollen cloth, which she should insert to a depth that the
male organ penetrates, and she should then see if there is any
reddish spot on it. If it is impossible for her to insert it to
such a depth, she should at least try to the best of her ability
to examine herself as closely as possible; and it is urgent that
at least one examination should be made to the depth that
the male organ reaches." This menstrual fetishism culminates
in the final proof of purity, the *mikveh,* a ritual bath in which
the woman immerses herself at the end of the twelve days,
muttering blessings the while, to emerge clean to the male
touch.

Lest there still remain any doubt as to the general uncleanliness of the female sex, it extends even to newborn children: a woman is ritually unclean for three weeks after a male child is born, and for double that time after the birth of a female child.

It would seem impossible to regard such laws with anything but repugnance. But the booklet *Happy Marriage*,[7] handed to every woman who registers for marriage, is almost admirably inventive in its attempt to explain their worth. Combining Talmudic sayings with vaguely attributed and highly questionable medical research, it produces such black pearls as the following: "It was discovered that the woman's blood in the days of her impurity contains a certain poison which could damage the man and the foetus. It is accepted that this poison affects fermented materials such as dough, wines and yeasts." Quoting "the sexologist Dr. Bernard Shapiro," the author, a *rabbanit* (rabbi's wife), writes that modern science now knows that menstrual blood is full of bacteria and "bloody elements" that are dangerous to man, and then produces what today is the ultimate coercion: "It is accepted by gynecologists that cancer of the cervix . . . is rare among women who keep the laws of *niddah*."*

The threats are psychological as well as physical. Having called on medicine, the *rabbanit* veers into psychology to state that women who do not observe the laws of *niddah* will feel raped when they have sexual intercourse, and may also become frigid. The reasoning is that abstinence builds up mutual desire, and that the enforced two-week "dry period" each month ensures that the wife will not be seen as a sex object by her husband. Marriage is a "perpetual honeymoon," since abstinence supposedly makes the heart grow fonder. This reasoning may explain why ultra-Orthodox men are among Israeli prostitutes' most regular clientele.

Artist Yocheved Weinfeld, who was married to an Orthodox man until her divorce in 1976, has explored the pornographic core of *niddah*. Using the *Shulhan Aruch* as her motif,

---

* Cervical cancer, in fact, is comparatively rare among all Jewish women, irrespective of observance of the laws of *niddah*.

she took off into her own interpretations of the laws, using canvas, collage, videotape and live performance—in the last of which she was gradually transformed from an innocent young girl into a tearful and bedraggled bride, gagged and shorn of her hair, humiliated, confused and servile.

Lively and attractive, with large smiling eyes belying a deep sadness, Weinfeld, who is now thirty, had been working for some years on the female body and her own reactions to it, in particular the vagina. "I was looking at the *Shulhan Aruch* last year," she told me, "and I discovered how wonderful a thing it is, how erotic this dry code of laws really is. The words themselves are so poetic. And suddenly I realized that this was my material: it was made for me, and I for it!" The eroticism lies in the concentration on the forbidden: "The text is erotic in an almost pornographic sense . . . the details of sex, the tension, the fascination. Sometimes I think of this Rabbi Caro sitting there alone in his room in Safed, thinking of and writing down all this fantastic material. I try and imagine what kind of a man he must have been, what must have been going on in his mind. . . ." Working through her own fascination with the laws and rituals, Weinfeld brought them out of the subconscious awareness of her audience and forced them into consciousness.

She was met with rejection and denial. "She's sick," said some of the women at one exhibition. "What on earth makes her want to talk about such things in public?" "It's disgusting," said most of the men, "all this concentration on menstruation—who wants to know about it? Bad enough that it happens, but to bring it out into the open . . ." By the style of their denial, such men and women, the irreligious avant-garde elite of Israel, reveal the extent to which they still breathe the atmosphere of Joseph Caro's little room in Safed. Although many Israeli women intellectually reject the letter of the Jewish law, its emotional impact is internalized from an early age, degrading their self-image. As Weinfeld says, "You don't release yourself from this sort of thing so quickly. It passes on from mother to daughter to daughter."

Orthodox Judaism is therefore far more than a religion

in Israel today. It is a code of law that is particularly restrictive for women; it is a civilly binding force; and it constitutes a political power bloc that can effectively quash any legislation for real sexual equality. But more important still, it constitutes a moral system whose values and attitudes penetrate the consciousness of every Israeli, man and woman, religious and nonreligious.

This is the Judaic yoke. It has been affirmed throughout the centuries, and every day in this century, by religious men who chant the daily blessing thanking God for having created them male and not female. And it has been given the force of law by the modern State of Israel with its transference of complete control of marriage and divorce to the Orthodox religious establishment, which imposes its view of women as men's property and as a means to continuity of the Jewish people. Two legal systems—the secular and the religious—operate side by side and clash on a number of points, from marriage age of polygamy. Thus the State of Israel is in effect paying religious and rabbinical functionaries to work against its own civil laws. Instead of imposing the twentieth century on the primitive religious legal system, the secular state is helpless before this Golem which it helped create. And Israeli women are the main victims.

Only twenty-two percent of Israelis see themselves as religious (in a survey conducted for the Ministry of Religious Affairs).[8] And the religious political parties control only 12½ percent of Knesset seats. Yet this religious minority has imposed the Judaic yoke on the rest of the country. It was not as difficult a process as one might suppose, for the sad truth is that Israel accepts this yoke since it gives concrete expression to an emotional identification with Judaism.

Forty-two percent of Israelis define themselves as "traditional." Though they do not obey the letter of the Jewish law, they sympathize with and derive comfort from the religion, and would not dream of changing its legal status. Many others have a more diffuse identification with Judaism, as outlined by Norman Zucker in his discussion of Israeli "theo-politics": "Much of Israeli nationalism builds on biblical and religious roots and is a response to historic persecution. So while many Israeli secularists might resist Orthodox restrictions imposed on the non-religious, there remains a widespread and deep-rooted attachment to Judaism which is an integral part of the Israeli civic awareness."[9]

Many Israelis are hardly aware of this emotional identification. In a way, they are pagan Jews, emotionally involved with the religion but intellectually remote from it. Like it or not, knowingly or not, they have suckled on the religion throughout their lives, derived comfort from it, used it when necessary and discarded it, if possible, when inconvenient.

The Bible is an integral part of any Israeli youngster's education. It is taught in the highly centralized school system as history, as literature and as geography, as well as being the basis of lessons on Jewish consciousness and religion. It is the guidebook for many of the *tiyulim* (trips) taken by bus- and truck-loads of school youth around this tiny country, following the tracks of this or that figure in the Bible, visiting battlefields and sites of various other biblical events. It provides the impetus for Israel's national hobby—archeology. It is the source of the first names of at least half the children born in Israel, and provides strong figures for identification.

Israel is the land where the Bible, and Judaism, often make sense. The Jewish New Year falls at the end of Israel's long dry summer, when the earth is parched and cracked and any grasses left unwatered have long since turned brown and crackled. Sometimes the minor miracle occurs of the first rain falling on the day of the New Year itself, a sign that the drought is over and that all is to be renewed and refreshed by fall and winter. The very timing of the Jewish New Year, in Israel, has a significance that the midwinter Christian New Year does not have. It means rain, renewal of the annual cycle, and thus in the most practical sense a new year started. Passover, the time when Jews all over the world sit down to celebrate the exodus from Egypt under Moses, also has a very special meaning in Israel, a country which has been through five wars with Egypt in less than thirty years.

All but one of Israel's national festivals—Independence Day—are rooted in Judaism. The sense of modern Israel as a continuation of biblical and apocryphal history, even to the extent of calling the modern Israeli nation the Third Jewish Kingdom, lends a special significance to such days of mourning as *Tisha be'av* (the Ninth of Av), the day of the destruction of the Second Temple and the day on which the Messiah will reportedly be born.

Everything, of course, is in the language of the Bible—a vital symbol of the rejuvenation and re-creation of the Jewish people in their own land. The Hebrew language, crude but vibrant in its everyday use, also symbolizes an escape from what Israelis see as the downtrodden subservience of the Yiddish-speaking Jews of Eastern Europe, or of the Ladino and Arabic speakers of North Africa and the Middle East, throughout the last two thousand years. There is a pride in the Hebrew language stemming paradoxically from a dual sense of historic continuity and historic break.

But where rites of passage are concerned, there is no historic break. In addition to the forced acquiescence to religious marriage and divorce, Israelis willingly undertake the main Jewish rituals for life events. The brith milah (circumcision), the bar mitzvah at age thirteen, the kaddish said over the grave of a dead father by his son—all are male rituals, all rituals which no Israeli would dream of forgoing, and all rituals in which there is no place for women. While the male child is welcomed into the community with the brith milah, the female child is often greeted with the wish *mazal le-banim* (good luck for sons), the appearance of a girl apparently being assurance of a boy next time, the laws of probability notwithstanding. Every thirteen-year-old boy goes through the bar mitzvah; and although twelve-year-old girls have now started the bat mitzvah, patterned after custom in the Reform and Conservative communities in the States, it is but a poor imitation of the male ritual. Only sons or male relatives are allowed to say kaddish for a dead father, and any father without a son is regarded as an unfortunate, for without the kaddish prayer over his grave his soul may have to wander. In a country where state funerals for soldiers are all too common, this emphasis on the community of males, even in death, takes its toll of women's self-image.

Jewish identity is of prime importance to Israelis. Hebrew University psychologist Simon Herman, whose studies show that Israelis see Jewishness and Israeliness as inextricably interrelated,[10] notes that as an Israeli, the Israeli Jew has a very short-lived past, while as a Jew, his time perspective spans thousands of years.

The Israeli identity, less than thirty years old, is based on the existence of a small and beleaguered nation still wavering between pre- and post-industrialism. It is a harsh country to live in, its population among the most heavily taxed in the world, and its per capita income far lower than in most Western countries. As Moses' spies reported to him on returning from a scouting expedition, thousands of years ago, it is "a country that devours its inhabitants"—a phrase much repeated by modern Israelis whenever taxes are raised yet again, or terrorists attack, or another politician goes under in Israel's incestuous domestic political wars. The Jewish identity adds to and complements the Israeli one, at times enriching it with a culture thousands of years old, and at others stultifying it with a system of laws and messianic daydreams derived from the political and territorial aspirations of a Bronze Age desert tribe.

Even irreligion in Israel is often no more than a superficial reaction against religion, expressing the individual's attachment to Jewish law as clearly as the strictest observance of it. Some Israelis will demonstratively drive miles to buy bread from Arab bakeries during Passover, when only matzo (unleavened bread) is available in most places. Others will go down to the beach to have a cookout with bacon on Yom Kippur, the national fast day. Still others will come dancing out of the Rabbinate excitedly explaining how they tricked the rabbis by lying about when the bride had last menstruated (Jewish law stipulates that a couple must marry only when the bride is at the fertile height of her cycle). This pride in what is known as "screwing the Rabbinate" takes the system for

granted, however. The rejection is in vain as long as it re-
stricts itself to prankishness within the system instead of demanding that the system be changed.

Judaism prevails because it has provided, and still provides, the mainspring of Israel's energy. Young paratroopers
who had never been openly religious wept—a rare act for any
Israeli man, and all the more so for the toughest of them, the
paratroopers—when they reached the Western Wall in the
Old City of Jerusalem in 1967. The radio announcer reporting that the Israelis had reached the Wall was himself in
tears. Yitzhak Rabin, then Chief of Staff of the Israel Defense
Forces, emphasized the symbolism of the scene, which "revealed as though by a flash of lightning truths that were
deeply hidden," in his famous Mount Scopus speech at the
end of June 1967.[11] This imposing wall of huge hand-hewn
stone blocks, significant to the religious as the remaining wall
of the Second Temple compound, had yet a greater significance for all Israelis, religious and nonreligious. It signified
a homecoming after years of exile: not the years between 1948
and 1967, when access to the Wall was cut off for Jews, but
the hundreds and thousands of years it took to bring about
a deeper sense of Jewish homecoming and fulfillment. It was
the Wall which triggered the pent-up emotion—the sorrow
and pain of war and the joy of victory—transforming it into
a sense of belonging and proud identity, signified in the
rapid change of name from Wailing Wall to Western Wall.
Yet it was the State of Israel which partitioned access to the
Wall for men and women for the first time. Whereas before
1948 both sexes mingled freely at the Wall, there were few
in the Israel of 1967 who questioned its partition into a small
section solely for women and a large one solely for men.

A key factor in the transformation of Judaism into Israel's
national culture, and an ever-present element in the content
of Jewish identity for Israelis, is the Holocaust—the name so
carefully chosen to express the sheer horror, almost beyond
human comprehension, of the slaughter of the Jews under the
Nazis. The State of Israel was founded only three years after
the concentration camps were liberated, only three years after

the details and scope of the atrocities became clear. The six million Jews who died were killed not because they were religious, but because they were ethnic Jews. Three years later, it was vital for close to a million Jews in Israel to stand up and identify themselves as Jews in every sense of the word. It was vital—not because of a great love of the Jewish religion, but because of the gut reaction to the destruction of over a third of the world's Jews—to rebuild the Jewish people and create it anew in a new land, with full consciousness and pride in being Jewish.

Power politics constituted the practical reason for the new State of Israel's decision to institutionalize the Orthodox Jewish religion. But it was the sheer emotional impact of the Holocaust which allowed the new State to make its peace with this solution to its domestic political problems. The "historic partnership" that developed between the leading Labor political establishment and the National Religious Party was as much emotional as political. The presence of the religious gave the formal stamp of Judaism to the State of Israel, a concrete Jewishness defined not by feelings of be-longing or identity, but by cut-and-dried laws, rules and reg-ulations.

The trade-off was a basic one. The secular section of the government coalition would agree to religious control of mar-riage, divorce and personal status, and the religious would give their vote to the main coalition partners on most other issues. But beyond the realities of power politics—the dif-ficulty of forming a government in Israel that can get effective legislation through the Knesset—is a kind of emotional black-mail on the part of the religious establishment. The message is: "You Israelis cannot abandon your Jewishness, you have suffered for it and now must make good for it, and you need us to keep you Jewish, to give you the outward signs of the religion by which to define yourselves and maintain your identity."

So Israel clings to the surface of Judaism, to the dry dogma of the theopolitic which is the only clear-cut definition of Jewishness that most Israelis can find. Jewish identity is an integral part of the past and present of Israel. It is the existential reason for Israel's nationhood. But the expression of that identity is a sorry matter. "Israel today isn't a Jewish state, it's a state of Jews," says Rabbi Adin Steinsalz, the brilliant Talmudic scholar who heads the Shefa Institute for Jewish Studies in Jerusalem. "It can be a Jewish state only if the people in it have a Jewish life and a Jewish culture, if they are people who live and see things as Jews. . . . The character of the state depends on the people in it. Right now it has a problem of identity. In a sense it doesn't want to be a Jewish state, and so it takes the easy way out by leaning on the law as if it were a *teudat kashrut* [certificate of being kosher]."

This law—as expressed in the Law of Return and in the Rabbinical Courts Jurisdiction (Marriage and Divorce) Law—provides the external trappings of Jewishness. By clinging to it, Israel persuades itself that it is still Jewish, despite and even because of the fact that the vast majority of its population is not strictly religious. For, as Steinsalz says, this is the easy way out. It is the means by which Israelis gain a sense of continuity with the past and rationalize their existence as Jews in a state of their own. If by stressing the externals of Judaism Israel completely forgoes the vast body of wisdom and humanity which can be found throughout thousands of rabbinical writings spanning thousands of years, it does so because these—the heart of Judaism, its life and spirit—are for the most part lost to modern Israelis. The external definition exacts its price, particularly from women, but it is generally considered worthwhile, since it allows Israelis to define themselves as Jews and get on with the business of living a non-Jewish life.

"If the state was sure of its Jewishness, it could permit itself to change the laws," says Steinsalz. "The trouble is that the state has other things to deal with, priorities which demand immediate attention. Its identity as Jewish is basically a philosophical problem, and the state has no time for philosophy with security on its hands. So it's extemporizing."

This extempore concept of Judaism, Steinsalz believes,

is what has kept the National Religious Party in power, and what gives Judaism a negative chauvinistic character instead of a positive character. A philosophical problem, but one which translates into antidemocratic practice. When a woman cannot give evidence in courts that deals with her personal life, when she cannot be a judge in these courts, when she is discriminated against as a woman in their everyday rulings, and when she is regarded by these courts as property, then democracy in Israel is a male concept applying only to men.

The question is not one of definition, as in the "Who is a Jew?" issue, but of the content of Judaism. It concerns the heart, not the boundaries, of Jewishness. But the politicization of Judaism in Israel has inevitably led to a concentration solely on the boundaries, on the tenets of the theopolitic which has consistently blocked any advance on legislation for women. In 1975 a bill providing for equal rights for women was stopped by the National Religious Party's threat to resign from the government coalition. Similarly, the National Religious Party blocked repeated bills for civil marriage in 1975 and 1976, limited the extent of the abortion law reform in 1977, blocked the appointment of Golda Meir to the mayoralty of Tel Aviv in 1955 and attempted to stop her from becoming prime minister,* and gained monopolistic control over marriage and divorce. It made a farce out of the Equal Rights for Women Law in 1951, and it has played a considerable role in limiting women's participation in the Israel Defense Forces.

Civil rights is a heavy price to pay for Jewish identity, and it is Israeli women who are bearing the burden of payment.

---

* Due to the exigencies of the time, a halachic rationalization was found for Meir's being premier. A woman may not be "king over all the people." But the rabbis reasoned that since it is the president and not the premier who is "king," Meir was acceptable. It was a judgment she might have appreciated fourteen years earlier in Tel Aviv.

How heavy this burden is, and how painful, is perhaps fittingly expressed by a religious poet, Zelda, in her poem "The Wicked Neighbor." The neighbor, the "crazy lady," might be the Jewish woman who dares raise her head and demand that she be recognized as a person, and whose challenge all are too timid or too threatened to meet. Perhaps Zelda herself, as we see at the end of the poem,[12] had once tried to raise her voice in this very demand, only to be intimidated into silence—except for her poems.

> ... on the eve of Passover,
> when they burnt the leaven
> in every yard
> and a flake of soot blew over
> and soiled her dress,
> she pounced at me
> and accused me, quick as a bolt of lightning,
> in tears:
> 'You, standing over there—'
> she shouted,
> 'You do not care about me,
> my dress is soiled and you say nothing!
> Look at me—
> I am sick, very sick and full of despair.'
>
> A curious complaint coming
> from someone
> who had moved in yesterday.
> A strange and bold and fresh complaint.
> Deep within me my soul kissed
> her mad longing for gentleness,
> her unbridled, lawless longing,
> destructive as an earthquake.
>
> Her mouth was hell—
> when she opened the door, the children hid,
> and neighbors slipped inside.
> Her cold laughter haunted
> our decent existence that shone
> with the light of the seven days.

—Do not imagine that your goodness
is true goodness,
shrieked the savage laughter.
—Do not imagine
that your prayer is true prayer.
—Do not imagine that your courtesy
is true courtesy.
—Do not imagine that your joy
is true joy.
—And do not imagine that your happiness
is true happiness.

When we heard
that she had gone to another town,
that the storm had passed and was no more,
we breathed a sigh, we opened windows.
Beat, beat the drums!
Blow the ram's horn!
Play the harp and psaltery!
Now we shall be left in peace.
Prepare the beds,
tonight we shall sleep.
When I saw golden flecks
in the eyes of the herd—
my heart was filled with loneliness.
I knew
we spoke of her soul, alive
and daily consumed by fire,
as if it were a stumbling block.
In vain had her curses spread
arms of smoke
to embrace our tepid souls
devoid of all imagination.
In vain had the wretched creature
waved her torn red flags at me
to draw me out of the enchanted circle of my being
and lead me to the hidden point of her existence.
I became one of the bowed women,
one of the mass of gray-haired women,
and not a trace was left in me
of that splendid courage.

3
The Cult of Fertility

"Increasing the Jewish birthrate is a vital
need for the existence of Israel, and a Jewish
woman who does not bring at least four
children into the world ... is defrauding the
Jewish mission."
                    —David Ben-Gurion
                    Israel's elder statesman[1]

Few Israelis know of the ancient Semitic fertility goddesses
Asherah, a mother goddess portrayed giving suck, and Astarte,
whose name was taken from the Canaanite word meaning
"womb" or "that which issues from the womb." Just as few
know that Astarte's consort, Baal, was a symbol of male fertility. His name, "master," derives from the verb "to take sexual possession," and it became the modern Hebrew word for
"husband" and "owner."[2] These Canaanite cults were sub-
sumed into the Jewish version of the fertility cult as presented
in the Old Testament. Here, all the great mothers, with only
one exception, were first cursed with prolonged barrenness.
    Their suffering was acute. "I shall die unless you give me
children!" Rachel told Jacob. But in compensation for their
suffering, they eventually gave birth to sons who were particularly blessed by God and destined for great things. The
exception was Jacob's first wife, Leah, who suffered in another

way. Jacob hated her because she had been foisted on him by her father when Jacob wanted her younger sister, Rachel. After seven years' hard labor, Jacob earned the right to marry Rachel too. Now Leah bore Jacob one son after another, and after each birth would say, "God has seen my misery; now Jacob will love me," or, "My husband will soon be joined to me in love: I have borne him three sons." But Rachel, the loved one, was barren, and therefore had to take second place in the household to her unloved but fertile elder sister. The power of fertility is the crux of the graphically described contest between the two to bear Jacob sons. They used hand-maidens, sorcery, trickery and their own bodies to gain, for the fertile elder sister, love, and for the younger, the status of motherhood.

Thousands of years after the archetypal story was told, the Hebrew poet Rachel Blaustein, known simply as "Rachel," modeled her childlessness and the suffering it caused her after the biblical stories of Rachel and Hannah, Samuel's mother:

> If I had but a son! A little boy
> with black curls and clever eyes.
> Just to hold his hand and stroll
> through park lanes.
> A little boy.
>
> Uri I'd call him, Uri mine
> the name is soft and clear and short,
> a bit of daylight, bright.
> My dark boy,
> I'd call "Uri!"—
> "My light!"
>
> Like Rachel, the Mother, still do I complain.
> Like Hannah in Shiloh, still for him I pray.
> Still do I await
> that day.[3]

Rachel wrote this poem, *Barren*, in the nineteen-twenties. Just fifty years later, modern Israeli Rachels have adapted the biblical fertility cult to create their own Israeli one. In modern as in ancient Israel, the childless woman may be seen, and often sees herself, as sad and bitter, a failed woman. Married couples without children endure social pressures to start raising a family. Unmarried women are seen as lonely and frustrated, their natural desires for motherhood having been thwarted by their lack of success in finding a husband. (Motherhood without marriage is simply not considered a valid alternative.)

Fertility is a national priority in Israel. The Hebrew for fertility, *piriyon*, derives from the word for "fruit," and is used alike for human reproduction, work productivity, agricultural production and industrial growth. Fertility is a means of production, of pushing forward into the world, controlling it, and turning it to one's needs. But most important, fertility is a means of production of the next generation.

Eventually you realize that outside Israel you rarely hear talk of "the next generation." "The younger generation," "the generation gap," "the new generation," yes—but all these expressions take for granted that there will be a next generation, that continuity need not be insisted upon, and that the issues concern quality and style, not literal continuity. In Israel there is constant talk about "the next generation": as if it were a new concept. And for Israelis it is. After thirty years of embattled statehood following close on the destruction of a third of the Jewish people, it represents a minor miracle, not to be taken for granted.

The "Isaac syndrome," the phenomenon of parental guilt at sending sons to risk their lives on the battlefield, expresses the fear of losing the next generation.[4] This fear eats deep into the conscience of all Israelis, who as a nation are far more aware than most of the fragility and tenuousness of life. Newborn sons are named after uncles, brothers or even fathers who died in the last war. Children are spoiled, cosseted, wiped, petted, shouted at, hit, educated, discussed and fussed over with an intensity that is rare in countries where their survival is seen as a matter of course. In a country where life itself is always on the line, the life cycle must be fostered and cherished lest it be snapped. The next generation is more than a personal miracle for those Holocaust survivors creating life anew or for mothers in their mid-forties who get pregnant again when they lose a son at war. It is a national event, a concrete sign that the Jews are growing again as a people, establishing their right to their land as natives. It is, in the most literal sense, the rebirth of the Jewish people.

The emphasis on physical continuity is part of the Jewish heritage. But it has been strengthened by Israel's volatile security situation. On the eve of Independence Day 1976, Clara Ginnis, an immigrant from South America, was killed by a terrorist bomb in the center of Jerusalem. She had given birth to a girl just nine days before. Her husband, who was with her when the bomb exploded, was badly injured and now needs repeated bouts of plastic surgery. Father and daughter face a tough future. Nevertheless, the reaction of a close friend of Clara's was: "Thank God she had the child before she died. Somehow that makes it seem less terrible. At least something remains to go on living..."

Some women "cover their bets" and have three or four children "in case something happens to one." Whether a terrorist bomb, a war injury, or a traffic accident, the risks are higher in Israel than anywhere else in the world. "You have the comfort of others if one goes," explains Edna, a Tel Aviv housewife who has three children aged six to twelve.

The surviving siblings of those who have been killed face their own problems. The hopes and pride in the dead child, idealized after death, often devolve onto the surviving children, sometimes creating intolerable pressures. Eighteen-year-old Liora, for example, is bitter and resentful. She fought a pitched battle with her parents after her elder brother was killed in the Yom Kippur war. She wanted to go into the army, but as the only surviving child and a woman she had to have their permission, which they refused. Guilty for wanting to live her own life despite the pervading memory of her dead brother, whom she had idolized, and smothered beyond endurance by her parents' protectiveness, she finally fled both parents and country.

Talma, a nineteen-year-old kibbutz mother, talked about her feelings during the Six Day War: "It was a week or two after we'd had our babies," she recalled. "Some of the girls said they were sorry they'd had a child. I was thinking all the time I'm glad I've got a daughter. It was in my mind right through the war. . . . Somehow I felt all the time this wasn't the last war, that history repeats itself and . . . really, perhaps we need lots and lots of children—we've just got to go on having children."[5] If Talma sounds as if she is trying to convince herself, it may be part of her confusion about her role as a woman in a country at war. Many Israeli women go through the same process, searching for rationalizations.

After the Yom Kippur War in 1973, as after each war, there was a mild baby boom. This time it was more pronounced, for Yom Kippur was a longer war than those of 1956 or 1967. It started with a very immediate threat of annihilation and it brought heavier casualties in a shorter time than Israel had ever experienced. Some psychologists explained the boom by saying that women had reacted to the shock of the war in the only way they knew: having another baby. But on closer examination there may be a quite different explanation. Talking about their reactions, many women who had "Yom Kippur babies" reveal that the desire for another child was less theirs than their husbands'. The men returned from the front in partial shock from the scenes of carnage and the sense of futility that followed the 1973 war. Many had experienced a violent realization of their own vulnerability. They had seen friends killed beside them and were painfully aware of how close they themselves had come to lying in the roughly dug temporary military cemeteries or being classified "missing in action." It was the men, suddenly brought up short against their own temporality, who insisted on survival: if not personal survival, then at least in posterity. Lina Wertmuller's hero in the film *Seven Beauties,* who comes home from a Nazi camp to make "more and more babies," makes perfect sense to such men. For death is a constant reality.

Eros and Thanatos, the Freudian constructs of life and death, create the dialectic of the life process. Israelis, though they would reject any such intellectualization of the process, live and work out these constructs by assuming that war and the womb are antitheses. The womb is life: personal life, and future life in the bodies and persons of created others. And if life has to be protected by death, as it does in Israel, then as much life as possible must be created before death—not in any magical attempt to ward off death, but in an almost conscious urge to render it meaningful.

The power of this transposition of Eros and Thanatos is not new to the Jewish experience of this century. "We Jews have done more than our 'share' for zero population growth," says Hebrew University sociologist Eliezer Jaffe. "It's time we started working on our own survival."[6]

One Israeli who was among the American forces that finally liberated the Nazi concentration camps in 1945 vividly remembers, with a mixture of shock and respect, the rush of male and female camp survivors toward each other and the sight of living skeletons copulating openly and publicly. It seemed to him to be an immediate reaction of "I'm alive," a reassertion of life in the midst of death. It was the primitive and irresistible proof of life by the imposition of Eros on Thanatos. Later, in the transfer camps set up for concentration camp survivors, promiscuity and pregnancy rates were high; the survivors simply refused the condoms offered by American soldiers. These were painfully and superbly human responses to death and annihilation, atavistic responses that arouse both admiration and revulsion in recognition of the indomitable force of this need for continuity.

On a lesser but more familiar level, many Israeli men relate how sex during overnight leave in wartime was an experience whose intensity could never be matched, whether with a dearly loved wife or friend or with a casual acquaintance. They were vaguely aware that this was directly related to the death and destruction that had surrounded them a few hours before, but often preferred not to make the link and shrugged off the experience with "Everything's different in wartime." Such wartime encounters were less sexual than mothering experiences for the women, however. Many women still describe the distance they felt then between themselves and the men. They recognized the men's need for comfort and reassurance of life, but their own experience of the counterpoint of life and death was a vicarious one. Many became pregnant not as a reaffirmation of life, but as part of the process of mothering their husbands; and children for them were less a means to immortality than solid human entities to be borne, raised, fed, clothed, eventually parted from.

The creation of the next generation is a cult that is rooted in a unique and overwhelming mixture of historical and emotional sensibility. The idol is not Asherah nor Astarte, neither Baal nor Yahweh, but the object of the gods' attentions—the womb.

"The womb of the woman belongs to the motherland," political satirist Amos Kenan wrote in 1974,[7] during the first phases of the struggle to reform the abortion law. Kenan was referring to the politicization of the womb in the central argument against reform, the argument generally known in Israel as "the demographic threat." It is a double threat. First, it relates to the drastic security problem of a country of three million Jews in continuing conflict with 150 million Arabs. "The Egyptians alone outnumber Israeli Jews by ten to one, and anyone who witnessed the human-wall assaults of Egyptian troops across the Suez Canal during the Yom Kippur War knows the importance of population for Israel's security," wrote sociologist Eliezer Jaffe.[8] While Israel has relied militarily on quality rather than quantity, there is an uneasy awareness that this will work only up to a point, and that this point is fast approaching as the technological gap between Israel and the Arab states, aided by the riches of Arab oil power, narrows. Second, and closer to home is the difference in birthrates between Israeli Arabs—at present roughly 15 percent of the population—and Israeli Jews. The Arab birthrate is far higher than the Jewish. It is this fact that was the focus of the infamous Koenig Report, prepared by the chief official of the Ministry of the Interior for the north of Israel, and leaked to the press in 1976.[9] (Israel Koenig predicted a larger Arab than Jewish population in Israel's northernmost sector, the Galilee, by 1978, and proposed a series of anti-democratic measures aimed at forestalling that eventuality.) The Koenig Report was disowned by the government, but it reopened the Pandora's box of the demographic threat, and raised the question—as yet avoided but bound to become a national concern in the next decade—of whether Israel can be both a Jewish and a democratic state.

The official presentation of the problem relies on statistics of population projections. It was first broached in the early 1940s, when David Ben-Gurion, Israel's charismatic elder statesman, climbed onto the pronatalist bandwagon. He was to become the high priest of Israel's cult of fertility. Disturbed by a Jewish birthrate of well under 20 per thousand population, Ben-Gurion called on Jews in Palestine to fulfill their "demographic duty" to the nation, and reiterated the appeal several times over the next thirty years. Demographer Dov Friedlander describes Ben-Gurion addressing Israel's major political party in 1943:[10] posing the question of whether the majority of the Jewish population did in fact fulfill their reproductive responsibility to the nation, Ben-Gurion said that an average of 2.2 children per family was inadequate and that such a rate of reproduction, if there was no immigration (at that time there was a strict quota on immigration, imposed by the British), implied that the Jewish community would gradually die out. He also pointed out that without a Jewish majority in Palestine a Jewish state—then "the state on the way"—would be impossible.

It was a valid point, and it still is. Friedlander estimates that the natural increase differential between the Jewish and Arab populations, together with longer life expectancy for Israeli Arabs due to the improvement in medical and welfare services since 1948, would result in an Arab population as great as the Jewish one, if there were no Jewish immigration, within three generations.[11] Statistics professor Roberto Bachi cuts the time shorter. Taking into account the Arab population of the territories occupied by Israel after the Six Day War, he calculates that the Arab and Jewish populations could be practically the same size by the end of this century.[12] In 1975 the Jewish Israeli birthrate was 24.7 per thousand population; the Arab Israeli rate was 44.6, nearly double. A pro-natalist policy, however shortsighted, becomes understandable.

Ben-Gurion envisioned a minimum quota of children per couple. At first he wanted "more than two or three," then eventually upped the ante to at least four or five. Though an official norm was never instituted, the government gave a certain backing to Ben-Gurion's pro-birth policy in the fifties by establishing a system of cash prizes for women bearing their tenth child. The system was quietly abolished in 1959—the majority of the women who received the prize were Arabs—but its spirit lives on in National Insurance child allowance payments, which take a sudden jump upward with the third child.

It was more than statistics that moved Ben-Gurion. When he first discovered pronatalism in the early forties, news had begun trickling through about what was happening in Europe under the Nazi regime. As the dimensions of the Holocaust became known, culminating in the horrifying revelation of its scope in 1945, shock yielded to determination. Ben-Gurion was not the most extreme exponent of pronatalism in his time. The two most extraordinary arguments came from the religious camp.

While Ben-Gurion's reasoning was nationalist and political, that of Chief Rabbi I. H. Herzog was steeped in a mystical sense of the Jewish race. Appealing in 1943 for Jewish families to have more children, Herzog suggested that the terrible fate of European Jewry was a consequence, "by the Will of God," of the modern style of living that had spread throughout the nation. (His rationale was to be taken up years later by ultra-Orthodox religious groups during the Six Day War: the outbreak of that war and the loss of life it involved, they argued, were God's "just punishment" of the Jews for performing autopsies in the Jewish state.) In his fanatically blinkered frame of mind, Herzog went on to attack contraception. He was supported in an equally convoluted and even more absurd manner by the Orthodox mathematics professor A. H. Fraenkel, who advocated total war against doctors performing abortions and quoted, in justification, Hitler's 1933 edict that forbade abortions in Nazi Germany, in order to increase the Aryan race.[13]

Hebrew University professor Yeshayahu Leibowitz, an iconoclastic and deeply religious Jewish thinker, remarked in 1966 that Israel's low birthrate was "turning us into one of the biologically decadent islands of humanity."[14] And a year later Ben-Gurion made one of his last public statements on the issue in the influential daily *Ha'aretz*. He expressed grave concern about the high birthrate in the newly conquered West Bank of the Jordan, and concluded that "a Jewish woman who does not bring at least four children into the world . . . is defrauding the Jewish mission."[15]

It may be that Ben-Gurion was defrauded by statistics, however. The basic statistics show a total population of close to 150 million in Arab countries, with an average population growth rate of 2.7 percent, and an Israeli Jewish population of three million, with a growth rate of 2.1 percent. They show an Israeli Arab population of close to half a million, plus an Arab population in the occupied territories of close to a million. And they show a declining Jewish birthrate in Israel, from 29.4 per thousand in 1949 to 24.7 per thousand in 1975 (still high as compared with 15 in the U.S., 13.9 in England, and 13.4 in Sweden).[16] But on analysis of these statistics one finds, as Dov Friedlander concludes, that even raising the Jewish birthrate to an average of four or five children per family would be meaningless in terms of resolving the population differentials within the next thirty years. Only political and social change, and not demographic change, can solve this problem; it is not the demography that needs changing, but its relevance to Israel's survival.

Despite the statistical and academic language in which pronatalist arguments are often couched, the arguments are nonrational and emotionally highly charged. They reveal an Israeli psychology tightly bound into the classic Jewish problem of survival, into the elementary, gut-level struggle of the Jews not to die as an entity. It was this deeply ingrained sense of the importance of national survival which kept the Jews alive through dispersion, inquisition, pogrom and Holocaust. But tragically, Israel, which was to be the solution to the problem of survival, is now one of the most insecure places in the world for a Jew to live. As political science professor Shlomo Avineri, ex-director-general of the Foreign Ministry, remarked in 1966: "From this standpoint, we (in Israel) are bearing the Jewish cross more intensively than any other Jewish community."[17] Israel has seen its past follow it into the present.

With so many ramifications to the demographic problem, it is no wonder that the Natality Committee, set up by Ben-Gurion in 1962 to advise the government on the demographic problem, only settled on its recommendations in 1966, by which time Ben-Gurion was out of power and working on his memoirs in the Negev kibbutz of Sde Boker. The committee was heavily pronatalist; instead of recommending limited family size for families living in substandard and often slum conditions, it proposed a series of impractical measures for financial support. Only one of its recommendations was put into effect: the establishment of a Demographic Center within the Prime Minister's office. In deciding to start the Center, in 1967, the government cited its aims: "To act systematically in carrying out a natality policy intended to create a favorable psychological climate, such that natality will be encouraged and stimulated, an increase in natality being crucial for the whole future of the Jewish people."

In 1968 the Demographic Center was inaugurated by Prime Minister Levi Eshkol, who emphasized the importance of increased natality for the Jewish people after so many had died in the Holocaust. The Center's director, Zena Harman, stated that four or five children might be the optimum average per family. The Center launched a series of publicity campaigns which, to its dismay, produced at the best a minimal and fleeting increase in birthrate. The affluent, faced with the choice between another child, a holiday in Europe, or a new car, clearly chose to enjoy themselves rather than fulfill their demographic obligations. To exacerbate the problem, Dov Friedlander was producing research results that indicated that whatever the reasons that Israelis had children, government policy was not among them. And then a series of research projects, funded and sponsored by the Demographic Center itself, came up with the constant that large families were strongly related to poor living conditions, higher crime rates, substandard educational levels, and the host of other symptoms of the vicious cycle of poverty.

The Demographic Center is in an untenable position. On the one hand, its aim is to encourage large families; on the other, by so doing, it encourages a higher rate of social problems and exacerbates those problems. Where the interest of the country would be served demographically, it is not served socially. The problem, as stated by a senior official in charge of the beginnings of a family planning system to be run by the Histadrut sick fund, is that "the wrong people are having the babies." The "right people"—the affluent, well-educated minority of mainly European origin—prefer material luxuries to maternal delights, while the "wrong people"—the close to 60 percent who are of North African and Middle Eastern origin, and whose average educational and financial level is far lower—go right on having children, since basically they have little choice in the matter. Professional contraceptive advice is available to those who can afford a private gynecologist or who are lucky enough to have heard of one of the experimental part-time counseling centers recently established with no publicity lest they incur the ire of the religious establishment. But for a large section of the population, contraception still remains virtually unavailable.

One might be justified in expecting the Demographic Center to disband itself. A strong family planning campaign would be against its own aims, yet clearly these aims work against the better interests of the population. By now the Center has worked through four directors, and is still quietly administering no distinguishable policy. In spite of its awareness of the urgent need for family planning, it has not come out publicly in favor of a nationwide network of clinics. Its first director, Zena Harman, who after a term as a member of Knesset is still on the Center's board of directors, says that the Center is now going through "reevaluation and reorganization of its aims." To what end remains to be seen.

Israeli women are less enthusiastic than the government about the cult of fertility, as the birthrate—from 2.6 to 3.12, depending on the statistical source[18]—indicates. Despite the official blind spot on contraception, women have held the birthrate far below the "desirable" level. They know what it means to be burdened by many children without adequate support, and they avoid it by any available means. In the lack of contraception, the main means is coitus interruptus backed by illegal abortion, the system employed by over half the population.[19]

Shoshana and I were next-door neighbors in Yemin Moshe the year it became the most expensive slum in the world. Built nearly a hundred years before as the first settlement outside the walls of the Old City of Jerusalem, the village is set into the hillside opposite Mount Zion, its red roofs and thick crumbling walls flanked by long flights of stone stairs grown with weeds. From 1948 to 1967 Yemin Moshe was one of the most dangerous places to live in Jerusalem; it sat just above no-man's-land, within range of Jordanian Legion positions. Those who moved into Yemin Moshe had no choice. Most of the inhabitants were Ladino-speaking immigrants from Turkey. Then the unification of Jerusalem, in 1967, put Yemin Moshe in the center of the newly united city. By the end of the year plans were being made to get the "native" inhabitants out and to turn the village into an enclave for the rich and well-known who were seeking summer homes in Jerusalem.

Shoshana arrived in Israel in the early fifties, married at seventeen, and was now a mother of six at twenty-six. Worry lines dragged down the corners of her mouth and knit her eyebrows despite frequent laughter. Sometimes on a quiet morning we sat together and talked on the stoop leading to both our doors, gazing out past Mount Zion, down the valley where infants were once sacrificed to the cauldron idol of Molloch, and over the Judean hills to the Dead Sea rift.

One morning, during a long talk which went through more than the usual cups of coffee and cigarettes, Shoshana wondered how she could avoid sex with her husband for the next three weeks. "I need some new tricks." She was going for her sixth abortion the next day. Her husband knew nothing about it. She did not dare tell him, since he wanted more children and would not hear of abortions. More, he would probably have beaten her for wanting to destroy a child of his. But the doctor insisted that after each abortion she must not have intercourse for three weeks. Five times now she had applied her imagination to warding him off for three weeks at a time. Now she was stumped.

As she talked on, Shoshana let it drop that the doctor had advised her not to have any more abortions, for she could only endure so many before she would become seriously ill. We got onto the subject of how she had become pregnant for the twelfth time when she had wanted no more children, certainly no more abortions.

"I've tried everything," she declared, waving her cigarette in a wide arc in the air, "and none of it's any good. I tried the pill and it made me sick, so I stopped that then and there. I tried the IUD and it hurt like hell, so I got another doctor to take that out. And the diaphragm? Well really, who can remember to put it in and out all the time? ... And then everything else—"ruefully—"really isn't much better than nothing at all, is it?"

Had she talked to her doctor?

Apparently he was not too easy to talk to. When he had prescribed the pill he had simply written out the prescription and told her to take them for twenty-one days, then seven off: no explanation of how they worked, no warnings of possible side effects, no suggestion that she come back and see him, that they might try another brand if this one was no good. The same went for the IUD: no warning of the discomfort she would probably feel during the first few days. He was a regular sick fund doctor, one of those who see forty or fifty patients a day and have no time for any of them.

"I can hardly go in and start talking to him like I'm talking to you, can I?"

Didn't he try to convince her that one method or the other might be easier if she gave it a little time?

"You don't see any one doctor in the sick fund. You just walk in and whoever's there that morning is there, that's it. Besides, they're all the same: they don't really care, and like they say, they're there to cure people, not to go round handing out contraceptives. . . ."

What did she feel about the repeated abortions?

"Look at me, I'm here, I feel fine, bless the Name. So another abortion, one more or less, what difference does it make?" She shrugged: "That's life."

And where did she get the money for the abortions?

Though not poverty-stricken, she and her husband had to be very careful with each penny. Shoshana waved her hands vaguely toward Mount Zion and arched her neck, "Here and there. I know how to raise it."

The stoop on which we sat is long gone, torn down along with most of the old house so that it could be completely refurbished and sold to the highest bidder by the government company that took over Yemin Moshe. Shoshana and her family were bought out in 1970, and we have lost contact. But I still wonder, sometimes, how many abortions she has had by now . . . and what she is telling her husband.

Shoshana's abortion record is not unusual: 46.7 percent of Israeli women have had at least one abortion by age forty;[20] many of these have had more than one, for it is common for women to have as many abortions as they have children. These repeated abortions, usually performed by curettage, increase the incidence of miscarriage. The fact that the majority of abortions are illegal does not prevent them being a major form of "contraception." Most experts estimate that for every live birth there is at least one abortion; some say that the abortion side of the balance is heavier.

The number of abortions in Israel is not surprising when you consider the findings of medical and demographic research: 70 percent of married couples use coitus interruptus for contraception, according to one survey;[21] according to another, 43 percent of married couples use no contraception whatsoever—and of these, 35 percent definitely want no more children.[22] But it is very surprising when one considers that Israeli women's ideal family size, as expressed in research surveys, is three or four children.[23] It could be that the abortion rate represents a concrete measure of what Israeli women really want as opposed to what they think is expected of them. In that case, the expressed ideal may be a compromise between the government ideal and the number of children that women actually have (an average of about 2.8).

An insight into the values and attitudes behind these figures is offered by sociologist Tsiona Peled in a broad survey of three groups: gynecologists and medical and paramedical personnel (the "suppliers"); women (the "clients"); and policymakers and opinion leaders (the "planners").[24] Her findings expose the welter of contradictions between intent and action, and testify to the persisting primacy of emotion in an area which doctors choose to categorize as solely scientific.

Although 30 percent of the general practitioners and gynecologists disapprove of coitus interruptus and safe days as contraceptive methods, they rarely discuss contraception with their clients. They generally do so only if the woman raises the question, and whether or not she does so depends to a large extent on her socioeconomic status and educational level. If these are high, she will probably go to a private gynecologist and pay for both advice and contraceptives. If they are low, she will see a sick fund doctor, get sketchy advice if any at all, and still have to pay for the contraceptives. Experimental family planning offer better advice and subsidized contraceptives. But meanwhile the majority of women, if they do try using modern contraceptives, do not persist.

The attitude of many gynecologists was expressed by the late head of Hadassah Hospital's gynecology and obstetrics department, Professor Zeev Polychuk. As the most prestigious gynecologist in Israel, he went on record in 1976 saying: "There is something inherently weak in the character of women" because they do not use contraceptives properly.[25] Perhaps he was thinking of a well-educated young woman who came to the hospital with a severe cervical infection two months after she had been given a diaphragm. Her doctor had not explained that she was to take out the diaphragm after intercourse, and so it had stayed in for two months— sheer stupidity on her part to Polychuk, perhaps, but in fact professional neglect on the part of her doctor.

The best-known contraceptive methods are the pill and the intrauterine device, but these are the least used.[26] Israeli women are less positive than professionals about modern contraception, and less negative about primitive methods. Their preference for abortion may be an expression of their distrust of the pill and other contraceptive methods. Apparently professionals see little need to ensure that the pill and the IUD be made available, and do little to help dispel women's apprehensions about them.

Tsiona Peled's research offers an interesting sidelight: the vast majority of women who do use the pill or the IUD have decided on the method themselves, whereas a large proportion of those who use more primitive methods report that it was their husbands who decided. The women are not happy with the situation: 91.5 percent want family planning clinics established throughout the country, and 93 percent said that there should be sex education in the schools. These figures include the majority of religious women in Peled's sample: she found that on all issues religious women are more liberal than the religious party leaders, and especially so on the need for family planning.

But one issue on which professionals, women and policymakers are united is sterilization. There are no euphemisms in use here to ease the impact: vasectomy and tubal ligation are both called sterilization, pure and simple. In Israel the term is weighted with emotional significance. It recalls so-called "experiments" in sterilization in the Nazi concentration camps; it conjures the image of the bitter and weeping Sarah, doomed to a sterile life by a barren womb; and it goes against the national mysticism of birth and rebirth.

Sterilization is practically unavailable, though Israel is one of the most advanced countries in the treatment of infertility. A multiple rapist may obtain a vasectomy if he requests it; a woman who has nearly died in Caesarean section and risks the same operation again may have a tubal ligation if she wishes. But if a healthy, normal couple come to a doctor of their own accord requesting that one of them be sterilized, the answer is no. There are only three or four doctors who will perform such operations on demand, privately.

Tsiva, a forty-four-year-old mother of four children, the youngest of whom is sixteen, could physically tolerate neither the pill nor the IUD. She spent six months scouring the country for a doctor who would give her a tubal ligation. Finally she found one through personal acquaintances. Other women search unsuccessfully. "You are too young," they are told, or "You'll only change your mind," or "How could you expect me to do something like that? Do you think I'm a Nazi?" Tsiva frowns as she recalls a Tel Aviv gynecologist, who is known for his liberal views: "You're crazy," he told her. "How could you possibly want to do that to yourself? Don't you realize how this will change you as a woman? You'll lose the very core of your femininity."

Professor Renzo Toaff, head of gynecology and obstetrics at the Kirya maternity hospital in Tel Aviv, explains the anti-sterilization stand: "As a means of contraception sterilization is wrong. To eternally cancel such an important asset as fertility without the certainty it won't be needed in the future is a disaster. We've had women with three children who've lost one tragically—we especially saw this after the Holocaust—and now they suffer the results of a hasty decision in the past." Toaff maintains that he brings objective factors to bear when he dissuades a woman from sterilization. "She's not thinking of the future," he says. "I am." Sterilization "is in effect taking away all a woman's possibilities for the future."

Behind this fear of the irreversible stressed by most gynecologists is a still greater one: the fear of murder. It is not murder of the fetus that gynecologists fear, nor murder of possible fetuses, but murder of the woman. When women are defined by their wombs, their existence is validated or invalidated by the use or rejection of those wombs. If "all a woman's possibilities" reside in her reproductive abilities, then deactivating her womb is existential murder. Rationalizations (women don't know their own minds, the step is irreversible, it is unethical) cover a fear of murder which is rooted in the definition of women by their biological attributes. Thirty years after the Holocaust Israel is bound into the biological myth in which the womb is not only the center of a woman's existence but also the core of personal and collective continuity. Experientially, tubal ligation becomes both murder of the woman and a step toward murder of the Jewish people.

Many doctors who refuse to sterilize women are quite willing to perform even illegal abortions. Lea, who is thirty-six and the mother of two children, came up against this phenomenon when she decided to have a tubal ligation. She had a bad gynecological history, could use neither the pill nor the IUD, and had been warned of the dangers of another pregnancy. A highly reputed gynecologist refused to perform the ligation, remarking that "in any case, with your gynecological history the likelihood of your becoming pregnant is extremely low."

"And if the odd chance comes up?" she asked.

"Then don't worry," he replied, "come to me and I'll do the abortion for you."

Although what he was suggesting was illegal, the doctor could easily afford to be open about it. Nearly 70,000 of the over 80,000 abortions each year in Israel are illegal. In a sense, Israel is a haven for illegal abortions. They are readily available; names of abortionists, most of them reputable gynecologists, are well known; and they are generally medically competent. Under a standing order from the Attorney General, illegal abortions are not prosecuted unless they cause serious physical damage or the death of the woman. But they cost the equivalent of one month's average wage—and far more than women's average monthly wage.

In February 1977, the Knesset approved a reform of the abortion law, scheduled to go into effect in February 1978.

The increased political power of the religious parties in the May 1977 elections, however, has made implementation of the reform a doubtful prospect.

One of the weightiest arguments in favor of reform was the fact that gynecologists are making untaxable millions on abortions, since they obviously do not declare illegal earnings to the tax authorities. Reform is largely a matter of the law catching up with practice. But in fact it may change practice in ways that work against women seeking abortions.

The reform was a compromise between the proposal for free abortion on demand put forward by feminist Member of Knesset Marcia Freedman in 1974, and the status quo, with the law divorced from reality and the gynecologists outside the taxman's net. It expanded eligibility for legal abortion on regular health plans to include such categories as single women and women under social or psychological stress. This last category may or may not be broad enough to include all women. That will depend on the professional committees to which they must apply. Women will still have to plead their case before a committee, and it is by no means certain that their pleas will be granted. The women carry the burden of proof of eligibility, and married women who cannot prove that they are under stress will still have to resort to illegal abortions. But because penalties for illegal abortions will be stiffer, the cost is expected to double.

The reform has aroused surprisingly little interest among Israeli women, with two exceptions: Orthodox religious women were organized by their men to demonstrate against abortion, and feminists demonstrated for free abortion on demand and against the reform compromise. Most women, anxious about the vagueness of the legal categories and their own chances before a committee, feared rocking the boat and upsetting the status quo of fully if illegally and expensively available abortions. The reform will complicate matters for women like Shoshana, who have abortions without their husbands' knowledge, since it stipulates that abortions be performed in hospitals. Doubtless such reasons were behind Tsiona Peled's findings that fully 52 percent of women who had abortions were against any change in the law.[27] Nearly half of all the women surveyed by Peled opposed reform.

The demographic threat was the most frequently used argument against reform. An Israeli woman's prime duty, as reflected in this argument, is neither as citizen nor worker, but as mother—up to a limit. Paradoxically, this limit is the number of children she has.

One of Israel's major domestic problems is the fact that the large families—referred to as *"bruchot yeledim,"* "blessed with children"—are generally the poorest ones, living in overcrowded conditions (ten people to two rooms, four to a bed, for example), and situated at the bottom of Israel's socioeconomic scale, with no hope of mobility. These families, all Oriental in origin, are despised by other Israelis, seen as troublemakers, and scorned for their inability to plan their families and their lives and make their way in the world. Often regarded as hopeless cases, they themselves have little hope. Many of the parents are bewildered by society's attitude toward them and by the lack of help from government and municipal institutions; having performed their demographic duty, they find themselves socially penalized.

Symptomatically, Zahavi, an organization formed in 1972 to work for the rights of large families, based its fight on the need for a larger Israeli population and the contribution of these families toward meeting this need. The organization has ignored the option of family planning. Zahavi's arguments are demographic—and demagogic. Its lawyer has even suggested that every mother of many children be recognized as an "approved government enterprise," just as factories in development towns are approved so that they may receive special tax benefits and grants.[28] From his viewpoint, reproductivity is as much a national asset as productivity and should be encouraged in the same way: while men serve their country as workers, women should serve it as mothers.

This stress on quantity has created a problem of increasing urgency. Almost a third of Israel's schoolchildren now come from deprived families, and nearly another third, although their home conditions are less crowded, are "culturally disadvantaged." As the problem passes into the second generation, those responsible for its creation continue to avoid its implications. In fact they are even compounding the problem by raising the notion of "internal *aliya*" (immigration from within the country by childbirth) as a solution to the decrease in immigration in recent years. (In 1975, for example, immigration and emigration equaled out at about 20,000 people each.)

Large impoverished families pose a vital question for Israel's future. It had always been assumed that as far as population is concerned, quality would follow quantity. Now that that assumption is challenged, a thorough revolution in policy is needed to ensure that the phrase "the second Israel," a phrase used to designate the underprivileged Oriental sector of the population, will become an anachronism. The means to this end is a clear planning policy on both the government and the family level.

The irony is that the embodiments of the cult of fertility, the very women who suffer the burden of large families and poor living conditions, could be the first to reject that cult. Many of them welcome menopause as a relief from continuous pregnancy, and would seriously consider sterilization if they knew it was possible. Instead of dreading sexual intercourse for fear of another pregnancy, as psychologist Esther Goshen-Gottstein reports they do,[29] such women might find that sex without fear of pregnancy can be enjoyable. Because they live under the heaviest biological burden of womanhood, these women, often referred to as "primitive," would welcome the chance to shake off the shackles of the primitive and deep-rooted biological myth and escape a life that leaves no time for embroidering such myths. For them the womb is the enemy, the source of death in life. Iraqi women told Goshen-Gottstein that they hated sexual intercourse "like death." Women in Shabazy, a slum neighborhood in south Tel Aviv, described their lives as being "like a prison," with no way out.[30] Those closest to biology know exactly how cruel it can be; they have few illusions of womb-status. The concept of the "privileged womb," now coming into fashion among higher-class women, is laughable to them.

The "privileged womb" is the counterpart to the womb as enemy, presenting femininity as a series of privileges that no woman could dream of forgoing. It is the metamorphosis of the biological myth into the myth of the "real woman." The ugly side of biology has disappeared; what is left is the special attention and protection accorded women by virtue of their being women.

Irit, at twenty-seven, has all the privileges and none of the burdens of her biology. She is the classic Israeli beauty. Tall and olive-skinned, with large almond-shaped eyes and hair sometimes loosely bound into a knot, sometimes cascading over her shoulders, she moves with the assurance of beauty. She comes from the Israeli elite, born into one of Israel's oldest and most prestigious kibbutzim. She left the kibbutz after the army—"it's no life for a woman"—and came to Jerusalem to study art and to marry. She has one child, aged six, who seems to confuse her by his sheer energy. Sitting on the terrace of her house in the Jerusalem quarter of Abu Tor, overlooking the silver and gold domes of El Aksa mosque and the Dome of the Rock, she talks about the privileges of being a woman. She is elegant, charming, childlike and feminine.

"As a woman I have a thousand and one privileges," she says, lazy and languorous. "No one could expect me to give those up. Here I am, looked after, cared for, pampered and spoiled. I have not a care in the world about money, I don't have to concern myself with such things as paying bills. I am free, far freer than a working woman, to do exactly as I like. I can paint, I can read, I can just laze around the house all day and do nothing: it is all my right. I am free of any pressures of everyday life. I have brought a son into the world for my husband, I cook a little here and there—and the rest of the time is mine, all mine. It's an enviable life."

While she loves her husband in her way, it is an affection based on habit and privilege rather than any deeper bond between them. He is the "simple affectionate husband who cannot understand her," whom Robert Graves advocates.[31] "A woman's task," she says, "is to be feminine, to be soft, to be protected by her husband. Men need a woman in life to protect, they need women to feel like real men, and a woman can't really have the leisure and freedom to find herself without a man to shield her from the world. So it all works out very well."

It may work out, but it does not seem to work, not quite. There is passion in Irit's life, one suspects, but it runs so deep that others cannot touch it and she herself, unless shocked into contact with it, is oblivious to it. She lives an arrangement of privilege and empty time.

Another proponent of the "privileged womb" is Golda Meir, the woman by whom all Israeli women have been judged, and who has lived a life with hardly a moment of empty time. Nevertheless, Meir, like countless other Israeli women of reasonably high socioeconomic status, sees childbearing as an unparalleled privilege. In fact, as she told journalist Oriana Fallaci, it is "the greatest privilege we women have compared with men."[32] And yet by her own account, both in her autobiography and in the Fallaci interview, her experience of motherhood was less a privilege than a constant source of guilt and suffering, as she found that she could have either a political or a maternal career, but not both. She expresses contradictions in her autobiography, writing that "being a woman has never hindered me in any way at all," and three sentences farther on, that women looking for a career outside the home have a much harder time than men "because they carry such a heavy double burden."[33]

Meir reveals only the tip of the iceberg, but its dimensions glimmer through her words. A woman's ability to bear children is the root of *all* the advantages she has over men— the privileges that Irit enjoys and that Golda Meir rejected in favor of public life. But not even Meir could escape the calculation of a woman's worth by the fact and quality of her motherhood. One of her special virtues as prime minister, in Israeli eyes, was the "motherly instinct" which led her to regard every Israeli soldier as her son and to develop the habit of making tea and cake for "the boys" guarding her house. When she abandoned her personal role of mother she became the national grandmother, giving constant cause for amazement, not that a hardened politician could also show grandmotherly virtues, but that such a grandmotherly woman could be so tough and intransigent. (And the psychohistorian might fruitfully delve into the question of a link between her political hard line and the soft line generally expected of women.)

Whereas women in the United States and elsewhere are now beginning to realize that their privilege is that of choice —the alternatives of sex without pregnancy, of love without motherhood—Israeli women are avoiding that realization. They exercise choice post facto, in abortion; but for them to take the full responsibility of deciding what they want before the fact is for the most part out of the question. Effective contraception is often seen as a threat: many husbands refuse to allow their wives to use the IUD or the pill for fear that the choice will be entirely their wives', not theirs. The wives acquiesce, since the status and authority of choice turn privilege into responsibility, responsibility that women tend to avoid and men tend to save for themselves.

The privileges of motherhood and femininity in which Golda Meir, Irit and other well-off Israeli women take pride are the burdens borne by Oriental women. The strong Oriental husband may protect his wife's and his own honor by beating her, for example. Feeding and clothing ten children on a welfare budget is a very different matter than caring for two children on an ample income. Feminine privileges carried to their logical conclusion are false, as almost any mother "blessed with children" can testify. Well-established Israeli women are merely turning existing conditions into privileges in an attempt to ward off the thought and decision demanded by life in the twentieth century.

The concept of childbirth as a privilege is reinforced by the fetishism of the "vulnerable womb." Infertility myths as well as fertility myths abound in Israel, revolving around such exclusively male activities—in Israel, at least—as driving a tractor, flying a jet plane, or driving a tank. All these, as numerous women of all ages and backgrounds declare, threaten the womb. Such activities can "dislodge your womb"; they can "make you infertile"; they can "give you malformed children" or "idiots and mentally defective children." The contradictions within this range of effects would seem testimony enough as to their origin, and the experience of those few women who have driven tractors or flown planes provides no substantiation for them. But young, well-educated women rattle them off with the same fervor and belief as the oldest wives. Malka, a kibbutz woman in her thirties and mother of three, is typical: ticking the effects off on her fingers as she goes, she solemnly says that driving a tractor "a. upsets your menstrual cycle, b. makes you infertile, c. causes stillbirths." There is scientific research to prove it all, she maintains, though the exact source and exactly where she heard about it escape her for the moment.

The "scientists" are also prone to such myths. Until the mid-sixties, army doctors would not allow women to parachute on the argument that it damages the womb. They were persuaded to change their medical opinion when the paratroop command decided that a couple of parachute jumps would not only be good for those women soldiers whose job it was to fold the parachutes, but would also present a challenging example to green paratroopers about to jump for the first time. The army doctors accordingly changed their verdict to allow women to parachute "under certain conditions," meaning that women working with paratroopers or with the air force might be allowed to take a jumping course for purposes of morale, with no danger to their health.

The "vulnerable womb" has even been enshrined in Israel's legal statutes. Where the 1959 Employment Service Law directs that there shall be no discrimination in the Labor Exchange's treatment of applicants, its second paragraph states that "it is not considered discriminatory when the nature or significance of the work" prevents application for or acceptance in a certain job. The law is a logical follow-up to the Employment of Women Law, 1954, which begins by declaring, not protection of women's rights as workers, but the following: "The Minister of Labor may, by regulations, prohibit or limit the employment of a female worker in any specific work, production process or workplace, employment in which is likely, in his opinion, to be especially prejudicial to the health of a female."

"A female," the law states, is not allowed to work at night. The reasoning is that she must care for her husband and children. But the law lists a slew of exceptions to this rule: "a female" can work at night whenever the work involves care of the sick, children, or the aged; she can work in customs, the police, meteorological stations, international telephone exchanges, prison services, airports, harbors, hotels and restaurants, newspapers (except in printing), "in managerial tasks," or "where the conditions and circumstances of the work do not permit the employer any control of the time when the work is done"—meaning night-shift work on spoilable goods such as dairy products. Thus there is no objection to a woman working at night when it suits society's interests. In nursing and service tasks, she is employable whatever the time of day, and in "essential services" such as telephone exchanges (which are run almost entirely by women) and food supply, her health and welfare suddenly come second.

The law means that most women lose the opportunity to earn the higher rates paid for night work, and some employers even turn away women because they can work only on day shifts. Moreover, women are not allowed to work at all in plants manufacturing acids, various other chemical products, or poisonous paints, or to work in contact with lead, lest these be injurious to their health or impair their ability to have children.* The womb is vulnerable, it appears, where the male gonads are not.

---

* Work under such conditions can harm the fetus of a pregnant woman. Both men and women, in fact, can suffer harmful effects on their general health and their reproductive ability. The answer to the problem lies in making work places safe, not in banning women from them.

The vulnerable womb is as pernicious as the privileged one. But since both concepts are reiterated implicitly and explicitly throughout her childhood and adult life, the Israeli woman internalizes them, often ignoring her personal experience and abilities in deference to society's expectations. The biological myth and its step-daughter, the "real woman" myth, justify her status by identifying her with her womb. In accepting these myths she assents to the elevation of a biological organ into a national, spiritual and social asset, to the extent that giving birth in Israel may take on the proportions of a political act. Protected by law and venerated for her potential issue, the womb's owner must be made aware of its importance lest she endanger an asset that happens to be lodged with her, but which belongs less to her than to the State.

4
Zionism and Manhood

Jerusalem:
"Thou shalt no more be termed Forsaken,
Neither shall thy land any more be termed
    Desolate;
But thou shalt be called, My light is in her,
And thy land, Espoused;
For the Lord delighteth in thee,
And thy land shall be espoused.
For as a young man espouseth a virgin,
So shall thy sons espouse thee;
And as the bridegroom rejoiceth over the
    bride,
So shall thy God rejoice over thee."
                   Isaiah, 62:4–5

The longing for Zion was one of the mainsprings of Jewish solidarity throughout the long centuries of dispersion; to act on that longing, however, was tantamount to an act of incest. As a mystical idea, the return to Zion afforded the bond of a future but "never to be achieved in our lifetime" redemption. It was imagined, as Isaiah indicates, in terms of the return of sons to mother in sexual union.

The sons were to rescue Zion from the "multiple harlotries" described by Ezekiel, to mount Mount Zion in the role of rescuer and sexual claimant, the young groom returning to claim his bride, the son his mother. The result of the inter-course between son and mother would be the rebirth of the son himself, who would give new life to his mother by saving her from the iniquities of suffering under foreign rule and restore her innocence and light as mother and life giver. It is thus little wonder that the fiercest enemies of Zionism in the early years of this century were the religious leaders of Eastern European Jewry.

Those who left their homes to come to Palestine in search of new life were the young, already in rebellion against their natural parents and open to another kind of filial re-lationship. Influenced by the new socialist theories making headway in Europe at that time, they found the courage to act on the longing for Zion. Daring and idealistic, they formed the "second *aliya*," the wave of immigration from 1902 to 1914 which formed the backbone of socialist Zionism, and the "third *aliya*," from 1918 to 1922, which consolidated what the second *aliya* had started.

Their courage was challenged by the shock of awakening to a far harsher reality in the promised land than they had imagined. It was a reality of malaria, barren soil, rocks and thorns; of a harsh climate, none-too-friendly neighbors, and open hostility from the elitist and anti-idealistic members of the first *aliya*, by now well established in the classic colo-nizing role; and of the sudden loneliness of being away from home in completely strange surroundings.

This was no welcoming bride, no old-new virgin mother waiting to be fertilized by her homecoming sons, but a bar-ren and unwelcoming country which returned devotion with sickness and love with starvation. So it was, perhaps, almost of necessity that these early settlers should return, consciously or subconsciously, to the metaphors of Isaiah and Ezekiel. They had to find a way to reconcile their everyday toils and troubles with their idealism, and the union and rebirth metaphor provided the ideal link. The contradiction between union with the mother and rebirth out of her was lost in the structural transformation of cruel bride into life-giving mother. This is an archetypal transformation: as anthropologist Edward Leach indicates in *Culture and Communication*,[1] mystical rebirth is one way of reconciling the holiness of the virgin in distress with the sinful sexuality of the new bride. By converting virgin into mother in a metabiological leap, sexuality is sanctified and defused, and past and present harlotries and betrayals are absolved in praise of the new life resulting from the union.

Aflame with a sacred if secular zeal to "make the desolate land bloom"—one of their main slogans—the young pioneers sang of their coming to the land "to rebuild it and to be rebuilt." Far more than a personal endeavor, this rebuilding signified both a personal and a group homecoming, a return to the womb of history in the form of the "espoused" —Zion.

The charismatic socialist Zionist leader Meir Yaari, guru of the commune of Bittania near the Sea of Galilee, was unafraid to express the sexuality of their zeal. The land they tilled, he said, was their bride, and they themselves "the bridegroom who abandons himself in his bride's bosom... thus we abandon ourselves to the motherly womb of the sanctifying earth."[2]

"Mother Zion, after being made love to by her 'homecoming' sons, gave birth to new life," interprets psychohistorian Jay Gonen. "Thus, the children replaced their father, husbanded their mother, and fathered themselves. They therefore experienced a Zionist 'rebirth' in which they played the new and masterful role of the potent life giver."[3]

But while Zion played Jocasta to the male pioneers' Oedipus, where was the Agamemnon for the women pioneers' Electra? What value could all this libidinous attraction have for them? What archetypal images could it arouse in a woman's mind? What role was there for women in this scenario of sons and fathers fertilizing the motherland?

The mysticism of tilling the soil, plowing mother earth to implant seed in her and make her fruitful once more, was exclusively male. And its masculine bias was natural to a generation born and bred in the shtetl and exposed, in the Jewish Enlightenment of the time, to such influences as

Freud, Nietzsche and Weininger,* with their stereotyped images of woman as passive receptacle, contaminating weakness, or base necessity. Their overlay of socialism, with its credo of equality, was powerless against a deeply entrenched psychology of sexism and the men's painful sense of unmanliness to be redeemed.

"I'm opposed to Jewish history," declares Yudka in Haim Hazaz's short story "The Sermon." "What is there in it? Oppression, defamation, persecution, martyrdom. And again oppression, defamation, persecution and martyrdom. And again and again and again, without end." The heroism of withstanding all that, he says, is "nothing but the heroism of despair" and creates a new kind of psychology—"a moonlight psychology"—based on welcoming suffering. "Zionism begins with the wreckage of Judaism," he states. It requires the ending of a history of weakness and suffering and the creation of a "different people. ... Please note that: not new or restored, but different."[4]

This people proved to be neither new nor restored nor different, but simply the reverse side of the coin that Yudka, and the pioneers on whom he is modeled, perceived. Instead of passive, accepting and weak, it was to be an active, forceful and strong people; instead of the feminine stereotype, it was to be the apotheosis of the masculine. The role change from Jew to Zionist was seen by the male settlers as crossing the line between unmanly passivity and manly action, from feminine acceptance to masculine assertion.

---

* Otto Weininger, an Austrian psychologist who converted from Judaism to Christianity a year before his death, influenced certain trends in both Zionist and Nazi thinking. For him, this would have involved no paradox. A rabid antifeminist and proponent of male superiority, he argued that women lived only for sex and procreation, whereas men were concerned with the "higher" things of life. Only Jews were worse than women in his scheme of things, since they lived for nothing; Zionism, to be successful, therefore demanded the death of Judaism. In 1903, at age twenty-three, Weininger performed perhaps the most rational act of his life: he killed himself.

Zionism was the ultimate masculine protest of these young Jews. It was, in Jay Gonen's words, "the Jewish reassertion of manhood," which "restored potency after a seemingly endless and depressing impotence."[5] But this psychological formulation excluded women. Their options were to "become men," or to remain with the conventional female roles of Eastern Europe.

Language only exacerbated the underlying problem. In itself a rebirth, having lain dormant for thousands of years except in strictly religious use, Hebrew gives expression to the national symbolism of sex roles. For example, the word for motherland, *moledet*, is a feminine noun derived from the verb "to give birth." Yigael Yadin, Israel's soldier-archeologist-politician, uses the word in exactly this sense when he described archeology as "digging into the motherland, back to the womb."[6] Like other Semitic languages, Hebrew involves the masculine-feminine typing of nouns and verbs, so that a toddler learning to speak must absorb sex typing at an early age in order to be able to communicate with the world around him, as well as to establish his own sexual identity. Thus a curly-headed two-year-old hung on to his aunt's leg as her friend addressed him in the feminine form. "You should be ashamed of yourself," retorted the aunt, "that's no girl, that's a *man*." The toddler looked confused.

Gever is the Hebrew for man, pronounced with the main accent on the first syllable, giving it an aggressive swing. The word also means a cock, or rooster. Since Hebrew is built around roots of three- or four-letter groupings, from which a whole range of related words are derived, the derivations of *gever* are just as revealing. It can change to mean "hero" and "heroism," and in reflexive verb form means "to overcome," leading to the incongruity of a mourning woman being told, with a comforting pat on the back, in effect, to "become a man." The Hebrew version of "We shall overcome" thus translates as "We shall become men."

But if heroism is purely masculine in Hebrew, weapons and fighting are even more explicitly so. While the sexual connotations of *gever* derive from the cock of the roost, those of weaponry derive directly from the penis. The Hebrew for penis is *zayin,* which is also the word for a weapon. The phrase for Israel's armed forces can thus translate as "an army equipped with penises," and the verb meaning "to take up arms" also means "to have sexual intercourse."

The concept of femininity in Hebrew is as clear. The word *rechem,* "womb," is the root of *rachmanut,* "mercy and compassion," qualities seen as quintessentially feminine; the Hebrew for "female" is *nekevah,* derived from *nekev,* "a hole or orifice."

Even the choice of Hebrew first names expresses clear role expectations. Those names that are not derived directly from the Bible often use biological symbolism. Thus men sometimes take the names of predatory animals (Dov—"bear"; Arieh—"lion"), and women of prey (Ayala—"deer"); men of trees (Oren—"pine") and women of flowers and fruit (Shoshana—"rose").

It was the Dovs and the Ariehs whom Arthur Koestler dubbed "Hebrew Tarzans,"[7] glorifying their newfound physical strength and ability to endure and fight on under the hard conditions of pre-independence Israel, while mourning what he saw as the loss of the spiritual and intellectual elements of the Jewish enlightenment and European culture. In his novel *Thieves in the Night,* the Jane of these noble primitives is not any of the women they live with, but the land itself. And in the contrived resolution of his plot, Koestler unknowingly demonstrates the male conflict between passionate union with mother earth and the earthly sexuality represented by women. The main female figure in the book, scarred by her pre-Holocaust experiences under Nazi rule, cannot tolerate a man's touch. The contradiction between her apparent sexuality and her deep-seated frigidity is resolved by having her multiply raped and then murdered by an Arab gang, leaving the hero to settle down to a calm life of companionship and occasional unemotional sex with the woman who wants to marry him, and free to invest his libido and passions in the Stern gang, fighting the British for the land.

Out of this image of the Hebrew Tarzans arose a new

one, somewhat more subtle but the more misleading for that. It was an image tailored to the needs of Israelis after independence, an image that would offer a new hope and a new ideal to the tired fighters of the War of Independence and to the refugees pouring in after the long haul of World War Two. This was the Sabra, the "different Jew."

The Sabra image came into its own after independence in 1948, when a kind of post-coital *tristesse* set in after the initial high of coming home to the bosom of the bride-mother. The honeymoon had been harsh and painful, and had cost thousands of lives through illness and fighting. But out of it all a new state had indeed been born, and as if to give it justification, a new race of Jews—Sabras—was to populate it. Native-born, never having known the suffering of exile or oppression and persecution, Sabras would have the self-confidence of growing up free and proud in their own land. They would be the antithesis of the stereotyped image of the Jew. Action and strength were to be their bywords; passivity and weakness were to be unknown. Impassive except on questions of their nation's survival, abrupt and self-confident with a free no-nonsense attitude toward sex, the Sabras were to know their own minds and, above all, would be freed of the doubts of constant self-questioning. They were to have their softer side too. Underneath the prickly, tough exterior of the cactus fruit after which they were named, they would be soft and tender. In fact, they would represent the ideal of the Jewish rebirth: strong when need be, tough and uncompromising in their relations with the outside world, but all milk and honey in their personal relationships.

That such a self-contradictory personality could hardly work mattered little at the time. There were relatively few Sabras then, a fact which helped to foster the legend of their attributes. By the time the first million Sabras had been born, the legend had been exploited in a series of potboiler novels and purportedly objective accounts such as Herbert Russcol's *First Million Sabras*.[8] Guarding the cover of the paperback edition of this book is a young woman, Uzi submachine gun in hand, apparently defending a desert outpost. Inside,

Russcol creates out of a temporary and minority phenomenon
—the ostensible independence and emotional self-reliance of
kibbutz and urban elite children—a new and permanent national type. His book is more a description of how he would
like his own children to be, one realizes, than factual reporting. And his description of women Sabras is a cheap
novelist's joy. In full control of their own minds and bodies,
free of sexual hang-ups yet with marriage and children real-
istically in mind, fighters together with their men and yet
soft and feminine when the spirit takes them, they are the
apotheosis of women as full equals and yet "real women"
for all that. This mixture of Amazonian prowess and irresistible sexuality has been glorified in movies such as *Exodus* and
Judith, and has reached the height of absurdity—and of
comedy—in the legion of Israel-based potboilers that hit the
presses in the late sixties, in the aftermath of the Six Day War.

The potboiler formula is simple enough. An uninvolved
observer, usually non-Jewish to avoid identity problems and a
journalist to ensure his detachment, arrives in Israel full of
his usual cynicism. Despite his better self, he falls in love with
the irresistibly sexy Israeli woman whose breasts are portrayed
thrusting up against her khaki shirt on the cover. She is
comfortably but unfulfillingly married, often to a soil specialist who is more concerned with soil fertility than his wife's
fertility. Drawn to the stranger by her sexuality, but almost
against her will, she makes love with him in the sands of the
Negev or Sinai and incredibly, without the sand getting in
the way, they "explode." As they explode, so does the Sinai
Campaign of 1956 or the Six Day War of 1967. She goes to
the front, ignoring all rules of the Israel Defense Forces
against women in combat. He follows her and, against his
better judgment, gets involved in the battle, performs a small
act of heroism, sees her killed before his eyes, and returns
home a sadder and wiser man, but with virility and detachment intact.

The perverted potentialities of making love and war together are exploited to the full. In one book, a handful of
women, breasts bare and heaving, take an Egyptian armored

column in the middle of the Sinai Campaign with plenty of dry-eyed hysterics, lesbianism and rape thrown in to liven up the fighting. In another, the heroine reaches the peak of her sexuality when she reaches into her shirt to take a grenade out from under her left breast and lob it at an Arab machine-gun nest. In yet a third, the woman, head of Israel's secret service organization in darkest North Africa, is actually called Sabra. She declares that her only lover is Israel—until the hero catches her off guard just before the big attack.[9] Eros and Thanatos are degraded to the level of sex and danger of death. But the conjunction of the two, even in this debased form, strikes a deep chord of response in male readers. The potboilers sell. For here she is: the war woman, all woman, the Amazon with two perfect breasts, the perfect lover fatal to all who cross her. She is fascination and fantasy for millions of men: the perfect masturbatory legend.

Famous masturbator Philip Roth debunked and rein-forced the legend simultaneously. Portnoy picks up the man-datory green-eyed, tawny-skinned soldier, "her small volup-tuous figure nipped at the middle by the wide webbing of her khaki belt," only to find that he is erectionless in the Promised Land. "And all the time that self-assured little lieutenant, so proudly flying those Israeli tits, prepared to be mounted by some tank commander!"[10] Portnoy—the victim of the great fantasy.

But it is one man, not these anonymous Amazons, who personifies both the myth and the reality of the Sabra: the Chief of Staff during the Sinai Campaign and the Minister of Defense during the Six Day and Yom Kippur wars, Moshe Dayan, now Foreign Minister. Credited with Israel's victory in the Six Day War, Dayan represents everything that war meant for Israel: a complete turnabout from the passive suf-fering Jewish image to the strong, self-confident and superbly capable Israeli image. Until just a few days before the war, Israelis were locked into visions of another Holocaust, tense and fearful of what they knew was coming, with a feeling of backs to the wall and no option but to fight. Dayan, ap-pointed Defense Minister a few days before the war, instilled a confidence and self-assurance that accompanied Israel until the Yom Kippur War of 1973. He represented the new type of Israeli: cool and effective, relying on the best of technology rather than faith that all will be well, quick to act with stunning effectiveness, and utterly pragmatic.

The black eye-patch became a symbol for those who wanted Israelis to be tough, realistic and militant, cynical and anti-ideological—Jews who "know the score," who have no illusions about the world. The Six Day War was their war par excellence: taking their fate into their own hands, choosing their time of attack rather than waiting for the inevitable, becoming masters of their fate rather than victims of it.

This sense of mastery was carefully cultivated. The Dayans and the generation of young elite Sabras who followed were trained for independence. But it was the superficial aspects of independence that were emphasized, the outward appearance rather than true autonomy. These formed the cult of chutzpah, a cult of impudence and self-assertion, daring and risk-taking, independent-mindedness and disregard for authority as such. It took a good sense of humor and a healthy dose of common sense to bring off chutzpah successfully, without its degenerating into arrogance and lack of consideration. It also took more than imitation of the outward manifestations of autonomy. And since humor, common sense and true autonomy are rare vitues by themselves, let alone to be found together, the cult of chutzpah extolled by various observers of Israel is well nigh forgotten in Israel itself. Nowadays the word is used to describe plain rudeness, and its cultish connotations survive only in the suffocating and rather noxious brand of perfume called Chutzpah, sold to souvenir-seeking tourists in awe of the legend.

Dayan is the epitome of the legend. Ready to flout authority when he has no faith in the person in authority, as he reveals in his autobiography, he was, by virtue of his brilliance in his field, very often borne out by the results.[11] Here is a man who can be an authority unto himself, who makes his own decisions irrespective, sometimes, of the democratic process. He is a man who made his very considerable mark in the most quintessentially masculine of endeavors—war. And he is a man whose masculinity has been demonstratively exhibited in a long series of well-rumored and thoroughly publicized affairs, one of which resulted in a roman à clef whose key was so obvious that it transformed a trash novel into a national bestseller.[12]

But it is also Dayan who shows the obverse side of the warrior-womanizer, the emotional cost of his highly developed chutzpah and masculinity. With two exceptions—his daughter Yael and his second wife Rachel, for both of whom he expresses reserved but sincere affection in his book—Dayan displays what one reviewer called "an echoing emptiness of emotion" in his personal relations,[13] with hardly a hint of warmth or love for the other people nominally close to him, including his first wife and his two sons. There is scarcely an indication of his feelings about the generals and politicians who march through the pages of his life. Pragmatically, he recounts deeds, facts, decisions, without really delving beneath them to reveal too much of himself.

The person who perhaps best understands the man Dayan is his daughter, Yael Dayan, who has written a handful of novels, all of them extraordinarily honest in their autobiographical descriptions and their picture of the real Sabra. "My father and I were afraid of emotion," she wrote in *New Face in the Mirror,* her first novel. "We didn't know how to express our feelings and thought it a sign of weakness to show them." And in *Envy the Frightened,* the hero is described so: "Do you know what he is afraid of? To be afraid—this is the fear that masters him, until all other fears, human, normal, healthy ones, are pushed aside and stop existing."[14]

Yael Dayan unmasks the fearless Tarzan of Sabra myth, and reveals the closed, emotionally frigid Sabra of reality, desperately trying to live up to the myth. Strength is his supreme value—not just military strength, but what he sees as emotional strength. This emotional strength is not the ability to enter into and to work through emotions, emerging strengthened from the experience, nor is it the ability to overpower by the force of emotion. It is, in effect, a ban on all emotional display. This accounts for the remarkably cut-off, emotionless style of Yael Dayan's *Israel Journal,* in which she meets and agrees to marry her future husband, Dov. Unless you are sufficiently acquainted with who's who in Israel to identify Dov, it comes as a shock when he asks her to marry him and she agrees, since up to this point near the end of the book she has given not a hint of any close relationship between them.[15]

One of Israel's leading psychiatrists, exhausted and even exasperated after the Yom Kippur War by the effort of trying to get shell-shocked soldiers to vent their emotions in order to bring them out of shock, mused that "to display emotions in Israel is to be weak." He himself was shocked to discover the number of Holocaust associations that came pouring out of these proud and strong young soldiers, and is convinced that the source of the emotion-weakness/action-strength syndrome is the deep-seated shame young Israelis still feel about the Jewish past, which makes them determined to "show the world" what a Jew can be: strong, self-reliant and above all masculine, active and assertive, given to no such feminine weakness as tears or emotional display.

Emotion, on any subject other than Israel and its right to exist, embarrasses high-class Israelis. On the subject of Israel, and anything related to it, they show the passion of a deep pride in their very existence. Joy, tears, anger, depression—all are allowable. But on any other subject high emotion is regarded as an unpardonable indulgence, an obvious sign of weakness and instability that excludes the emoter from the realm of acceptability. This embarrassment at emotional display, expressed in derision, is certainly one of the psychological factors behind the "second Israel" status of most Sephardi Israelis, who are unafraid to express high emotion either publicly or privately, in true Levantine fashion, raising shivers on the straight spines of the Ashkenazi establishment, on whom the Sabra image is exclusively patterned. It is also a major factor in the transformation of Israeli women into a kind of third Israel. Allowed and even encouraged to show emotion, women are automatically excluded from the main definition of a self-respecting Israeli: being strong and brave, "being a man."

Dahn Ben-Amotz, one of Israel's most popular authors, depicts a father, the son of a Holocaust survivor, talking to himself on his way to visit his own son at boarding school in the short story "Parents' Day." "Don't get emotional please —you used to say to him. You wanted him to be a man. No crying. You wanted him to be like you. You wanted to pass on to him your own revulsion at any outward show of affection. To love? Yes—but in privacy, with restraint, calmly, at arm's length. To be close? Yes—but not to be bound, not to cling." Remembering Kobi, the hero of his own schooldays, the father recalls "how I envied him, how I admired him. I wanted to be like Kobi—tough, strong, indifferent, closed up inside. I wanted to be able to feel nothing, just like him."[16] And though he never quite succeeded, the father learned to copy Kobi's behavior to the extent that now, when he really wants to communicate with his son and explain to him why he is getting divorced, he cannot.

The tragedy is well expressed by a psychoanalyst in Bruno Bettelheim's study of kibbutz children, *The Children of the Dream:* "Our children are ashamed to be ashamed, are afraid to be afraid. They are afraid to love, afraid to give of themselves. ... I am not sure whether it is a deficiency in emotion or a being afraid of feeling."[17] It is fear. Behind the strong front is the weakness of the fear of weakness; behind the fearlessness the fear of fear.

When this fear is momentarily conquered and the feelings do break through, it is accounted a weakness, not a discovery. Israel is a defense-minded country; it has to be. But military defense has developed into widespread psychological defensiveness. "I don't think people should discuss their feelings," Colonel Mordechai Gur, now Chief of Staff, told writer Elie Wiesel when Wiesel asked him how he had felt when his brigade took the Western Wall in the Old City of Jerusalem in 1967.[18] While Gur kept his emotional defenses up, despite the tears of his paratroopers at the time, many Israelis are sufficiently shaken by war to let theirs down a little—

not to the extent of tears but at least of talking. This is how *Fighter's Talk,* the touching and revealing volume of interviews with combatants right after the Six Day War, came into being.[19] The interviewers reached the soldiers before they had time to reorganize their psychological defenses, and the results were both human and humane. Two years later, however, in an attempted follow-up, most of the respondents, though not denying what they had said in 1967, shied away from that proof of their emotional depths. "That's what I said then, but I wouldn't say it now," was a common response.

This discomfort with emotions is masked by an ethos of pragmatism. The vacuum in emotional life is rationalized by a down-to-earth concretism that evaluates any personal action or transaction by its practical consequences. There is no point in emotional openness, as far as most Israelis are concerned. In fact, it can even be dangerous, leading them, as Amos Elon remarked in *The Israelis,* into "some vast unreconnoitered enemy territory too dangerous for loquacious traveling."[20] Emotions are risky, intangible forces over which no control can be guaranteed. And it is this loss of control that terrifies the Sabra, that invokes the specter of being controlled, and therefore persecuted, by others. Raised to believe in security rather than autonomy, in what is known and sure rather than the spontaneity of true feeling and thinking through, the Israeli takes the safe path of concrete results rather than risk his whole self-concept as the strong and self-confident Sabra. The myth has been internalized. He has to live up to it, and as a result, suffers the emotional impoverishment all too apparent in both the Dayans, father and daughter, and throughout modern Hebrew writing.

This emotional control bordering on frigidity, together with the adoption of pragmatism as a life-style, contributes to an ideological impoverishment among young Israelis. Their aim is to get the best out of what exists, not to change it, and values are based not on what is ideologically desirable but on what they conceive of as possible—a highly pragmatic point of view.

During an evening of discussion on women's status at the

Hebrew University, Sara, a science student, burst out with: "Of course it's not fair, but you can't change it. . . . What do the feminists want from us women? Things are hard enough as they are, but to go round trying to change something that can't be changed . . ." She shook her head in exasperation at the notion. "You can't fight nature," she explained. "The nature of women is expressed in where they are today, and you can't expect us to go against our own nature." Avital, who is majoring in social sciences, firmly agreed: "I can't change something just because I don't agree with it," she said in a reasoning tone of voice. "There's a reason why things are as they are, and if they are this way, then that's how they're meant to be. The reasons are in women's nature, not in society." The situation is a given, and ideology is limited to rationalizing the existence of that given.

This unthinking acceptance of what exists is encouraged by the Israeli school system. Hebrew University psychologist Kalman Benyamini, head of the School Psychological Service in Jerusalem, took a close look at what values teachers inculcate. He found an increasing conservatism among Israeli youth[21] and concluded that "schools may be tools for creating conformist 'good' behavior." "As a parent," he adds ironically, "I'm delighted. But as an Israeli, I'm seriously worried." Teachers give praise and reinforcement, he found, for a clearly delimited range of behavior which could best be summed up as "dependability"—the kind of behavior that presents no surprises and no shocks, which steers steady on a straight and narrow course, conforming carefully to expectations and, above all, causing no problems. "The students come out of this system very malleable," says Benyamini, "ready to adjust to whatever norms may prevail in society. It's the kind of system that fails to create internalization of values or personal autonomy."

Teaching within such a system can be a disillusioning experience. Amnon Rubenstein, dean of Tel Aviv University's law faculty, now turned politician, describes being a teacher as seeing "row after row of inkwells into which you are pouring facts that they pour back in their exams."[22] Shimon

Shapiro, a professor of environmental design in the Bezalel
Academy of Art and Design, sees his students as "sponges,
sitting there ready to soak up anything you tell them and
squeeze it all out on you again." The process starts early; by
age fourteen, when Israeli children finish the compulsory part
of their education, it is set solid. "You're not meant to be
sitting around here discussing things," students in a new class
at the Jerusalem Experimental High School told me, "you're
meant to be standing up there and teaching us!"

The implications for Israel's survival are worrisome. The
Israeli army has always prided itself on the initiative and
independent—often lateral—thinking of its officers. The first
major sign of a lack of such thinking, in both the political
and the intelligence sectors, was the blunder in evaluation
of intelligence material which led to the traumatic outbreak
of the Yom Kippur War. "What we're looking for in potential
officer material is those kids who've withstood the school
system," explains one army psychologist, "the ones who've
come through as independent thinkers despite the system, not
because of it." Indeed officers' training courses, within limits,
are one of the few instances within Israeli society where such
thinking is encouraged—but not for women, whose role in
the army is strictly limited.

Such independent thinking is fast becoming the exception in Israel, where the normality as in most countries, has
little to do with mental health but is a literal conformism to
the norms of acceptable behavior. Military endeavor is the one
exception, for Israelis are willing, out of necessity, to develop
different approaches to military thinking. But in all other
areas of life they aim to be perfectly normal—as like other
countries as possible, and especially those of the West, making
no independent evaluation of good or bad, desirable or un-
desirable. "Our nationalism is homesickness for normality,"
ruminates Arthur Koestler's hero at the end of *Thieves in the
Night*. Thirty years later, the situation has not changed: under
the highly abnormal conditions of constant threat to security,
Israelis yearn for the placid comforts of normality.

Poet Yehuda Amichai sees a normal world in terms of women:

> When after hours of walking
> You discover suddenly
> That the body of the woman stepping beside you
> Wasn't meant
> For travel and war ...
> You swell with a great joy
> For the world
> In which women are like that.[23]

Like Amichai, Israelis tend to seek out the security of normality especially in male-female relationships, since they cannot find it in their national life. Living at peace, without constant national tension, is a generalized and blurred concept scarcely comprehensible to most Israelis; but living as normal a personal life as possible provides a form of compensation. This yearning for normality requires strong definitive norms, however, and these are clearest and strongest in regard to sex typing, where they have developed into firm stereotypes providing clear lines for conformity and allowing a very limited range of variation.

The stereotypes are not unusual in themselves. But that they exist in Israel comes as a shock to the outsider. Throughout Israeli society—home, kindergarten, school, kibbutz, army, work—there are clearly defined role and behavioral expectations for each sex. The display of any kind of weakness or vulnerability is considered girlish or womanly. Young boys in tears are taunted by friends, parents and teachers alike for being "girls"—as are new recruits in the army who cannot keep up the pace. The stereotypes are learned very young. Researchers have found a shocking degree of sex stereotyping in the reading primers used throughout Israeli kindergartens and primary schools, running the whole gamut of heroic, gutsy, self-reliant, tough boys and fearful, admiring, unadventurous girls, boys helping fathers strip down the car and girls helping mothers in the kitchen, boys being active and girls passive. The primers also depict an extraordinarily limited range of occupations for adult women as compared with adult men. (In the main reading primers used, the three-year series *Mikraot Israel*, 144 different occupations are mentioned for men and only 13 for women, with mother, aunt and grandmother most often mentioned, followed by nurse, teacher ... and witch.)[24]

Such stereotypes inevitably influence the self-images of Israeli youth. Psychologist Benyamini has found strong differences in self-image between high-school boys and girls who were asked to rate themselves on a list of traits. The girls rate themselves higher for emotional, faithful, orderly, involved, merciful and warm. Moreover—a far cry indeed from the pioneer women at the start of the century who saw themselves as men—high-school girls today rate their femininity higher than the boys rate their masculinity, indicating that femininity is even more important to them than masculinity is to the boys. The boys, meanwhile, see themselves as more self-confident, more successful, smarter, healthier, stronger, more stable and more fit than the girls see themselves.[25]

These findings corroborate Benyamini's work on conformism. Psychological research since the mid-sixties has consistently come up with findings indicating that strong sex stereotypes are linked both to high anxiety and to a lower level of analytic thinking, creativity, and general intelligence: the perfect psychological breeding ground for automatism and conformism. Those men and boys who score higher than average on tests of analytic and creative ability also score higher on femininity tests, while those women and girls who are more masculine on such tests also show higher analytic ability, creativity and general intelligence. This move to androgyny, comments psychologist Eleanor Maccoby, a specialist in the field of sex typing, "does not imply that intellectual individuals are sexually uninterested in, or unattractive to, the opposite sex. It merely means that they share more of the interests and activities normally characteristic of the opposite sex."[26]

Strong sex stereotyping, and the fear of being labeled abnormal for displaying any behavior commonly associated with the opposite sex, should be cause for great concern in Israel. If analytic ability and creative thinking improve the more one is able to cross the barriers of sex typing, then Israel, which depends so much on the quality as opposed to the quantity of its manpower for survival, must seriously apply itself to lowering this barrier and encouraging both its men and its women to cross it freely and without fear.

So far, there is no indication of this happening. Quite the contrary, the stereotypes are becoming stronger. The highly masculine man is pragmatic, protective, assertive and emotionally tough, serving as warrior and husband, defender and father. His consort is the "real woman," very feminine, emotional and in need of protection, caring and mindful of home and family rather than country and people. The tenacity with which Israelis adhere to and aim for these stereotyped ideals betrays the amount of anxiety behind them; the intolerance of deviations indicates their power to threaten. In the long run, though the stereotypes provide a safe mode of relating and behaving, in which expectations are clear and no surprises are expected or accepted, they are self-defeating. Eventually they create the very anxiety and insecurity that they were designed to salve. The stereotypes are a defense against insecurity, but the effort of maintaining them is itself anxiety-inducing.

Conflicting stereotypes have aggravated the problems of Israeli women, whose self-image as Israelis is masculine, but as individuals is feminine. Kalman Benyamini came across this anomaly in his research on high-school students. All students rated Israelis as very masculine, so that the girls among them were in effect split in their identities—feminine as self, but masculine as Israeli. A mere matter of semantics, one might argue, were it not that in three vital areas of self-image (importance, strength and self-confidence) all the high-schoolers, boys and girls, rated *Israeli* higher than *self*. Assurance thus stems from being an Israeli—and this means from being masculine.

An Israeli woman is thus trapped in a double bind of

mutually exclusive options, and there is no way out within easy reach. She is caught between the Scylla of being an Israeli and the Charybdis of being a woman. To be Israeli she must conform to the male emotional norm, based on the concept of virile strength. And yet this norm does not apply to her. She is expected to be feminine, even though the more stereotypically feminine she is, the less Israeli she then becomes. If she deviates from the norm of stereotypic femininity, she runs a high risk of being labeled abnormal and therefore ostracized.

Dalia Rabikovitz, Israel's major woman poet, portrays a perfect conformance to the norm of femininity in her poem "Clockwork Doll," which recounts a dream in which she is emptied of her human self and transformed into an emotionless robot, incapable of feeling. At first the cracks in the mechanism show through, but she is made to conform and becomes completely passive, concerned only with appearance and nothing else:

> On this night I was a clockwork doll
> And I teetered this way and that way by fits
> And I toppled on my face and broke to bits
> And they tried expertly to make me whole.
>
> So afterwards I became a proper doll
> With balance and decorum in my habits.
> But I was a different sort of doll then; it's
> Like an injured twig that a tendril won't let fall.
>
> And afterwards I went to dance at a ball,
> But they put me with the cats and dogs: yet there
> All my steps were measured and rhythmical.
>
> And I had blue eyes and golden hair
> And a colored dress like the garden flowers you see
> And a straw hat with an ornamental cherry.[27]

The dream is not reality; it is the fear of what reality may bring about. Though neither Rabikovitz nor Israeli women per se are yet clockwork dolls, they risk the mechanizing effects of conformism in their sacrifice of logical consistency and of their own selves for the security of normality.

The Israeli woman of the nineteen seventies is in no better, and maybe even a worse, position than her grandmother fifty or sixty years ago. Like her grandmother, she finds herself cut out of the male guiding spirit of the country by virtue of being a woman. But unlike her grandmother, who attempted to resolve the problem by becoming masculine, she retreats from the problem by hiding behind a wall of femininity.

5

Sex and Security

In the beginning, woman's sexuality was not the source of sin and temptation, as the Bible we know has it. It was an integral part of her creation, a source of pleasure which was her right as an equal. This is the story of Lilith,* the first woman, created before Eve as Adam's partner:

> God then formed Lilith, the first woman, just as He had formed Adam. . . . [But] Adam and Lilith never found peace together; for when he wished to lie with her, she took offense at the recumbent posture that he demanded. "Why must I lie beneath you?" she asked. "I also was made from dust, and am therefore your equal." Because Adam tried to compel her obedience by force, Lilith, in a rage, uttered the magic name of God, rose into the air and left him.[1]

---

* This version of the Lilith story is from the *Alpha Beta di Ben Sira,* an alphabetically arranged Mishnaic commentary written sometime before the eleventh century. The author of the *Alpha Beta* drew on early Hebrew legends arising from the discrepancy between the accounts of creation in the first two chapters of Genesis. In the first, man and woman are created simultaneously, on the sixth day of creation. In the second, woman is created as an afterthought, so that man shall not be lonely. The discrepancy is attributed to a careless weaving together of early Judaean and later rabbinical tradition.

Independent and strong-willed, Lilith was a fully sexual being, unafraid of her sexuality, wanting satisfaction on her own terms. She is the victim of the first attempted rape ("Adam tried to compel her obedience by force"), who, unwilling to accept male domination of her sexuality, dared the forbidden by uttering the magic name of God, and left.

Why is Eve, a pale shadow, accepted as the first woman? Why was Lilith exorcized from the biblical account of creation, to live on only in little-known rabbinical and cabbalistic sources?[2]

The exclusion of Lilith was vital to establishing woman's submissive role in Hebrew and consequently Jewish society. It was part of the process by which the early Jewish religion differentiated itself from the fertility-goddess cults of the other religions of the Bronze Age Middle East. Judaism built the first exclusively male divine system, gradually editing out of its myths and lore the remnants of the other cultures within which it was born.

Lilith's sensuality, passion and independence were firmly shackled by their inversion into qualities of evil. For her defiance of the male law of God and Adam, Lilith was transformed into a demoness, a succubus and vampire who attacked men by seducing them in their sleep, using their semen to make herself fertile with hundreds of additional candidates for the host of demons, or sucking their life's blood and eating their flesh as part of her orgiastic satisfaction.

In her flight from Adam, Lilith found refuge by the shores of the Red Sea, "a region abounding in lascivious demons, to whom she bore children at the rate of more than one hundred a day." But lest the demographic balance between demons and humans become too lopsided, God's specific punishment was that one hundred of her demon children should perish each day. In bitter revenge, Lilith therefore preys on human children, especially on newborn male infants, who are particularly vulnerable to her until the time of their circumcision, eight days after birth. Unless protected by magic amulets with inscriptions such as "Lilith out, Adam and Eve in" and horrifying drawings of Lilith as a scrawny hag, used

until recently by Oriental Jews, the infant is in mortal danger.
In the *Zohar,* one of the main cabbalistic books, Lilith reaches
the pinnacle of evil by becoming the consort of Satan, the
epitome of wickedness and the forces of darkness. "Her ultimate vilification is man's vindication," says Israeli-born writer
Lilly Rivlin, who has taken the spirit and cause of Lilith as
her own in her quest for a Jewish mode of feminism.[3] Absolved of all blame for his inability to coexist with Lilith, the
witch, Adam was now free to establish his dominance over a
much lesser creation—Eve.

The fear of sexuality, the puritanism which stems from
it, and the concomitant degradation of woman, all revealed in
the myth of Lilith, are developed in the continuation of that
myth:

> Undismayed by His failure to give Adam a suitable
> helpmeet, God tried again, and let him watch while
> He built up a woman's anatomy: using bones, tis-
> sues, muscles, blood and glandular secretions, then
> covering the whole with skin and adding tufts of hair
> in places. The sight caused Adam such disgust that
> even when his woman, the First Eve, stood there in
> her full beauty, he felt an invincible repugnance.
> God knew that He had failed once more, and took
> the First Eve away. Where she went, nobody knows
> for certain.
>
> God tried a third time, and acted more circum-
> spectly. Having taken a rib from Adam's side in his
> sleep, He formed it into a woman; then plaited her
> hair and adorned her, like a bride, with twenty-four
> pieces of jewelry, before waking him. Adam was en-
> tranced.[4]

Eve One is a dismal failure: she is made of flesh and blood, a
physical being whose workings, including secretions, are all
too apparent. Adam cannot accept her; despite the beauty of
her body he is disgusted by the reality of a woman's physiology. What he wants, and what he gets, is the gift-wrapped
version—Eve Two—whose superficial adornments enable him

to forget her visceral reality and indulge in a romantic negation of her sensuality. The Adam and Eve myth is curiously
devoid of eroticism as it lives in the Bible; "they became one
flesh," presumably with her lying beneath him. Eroticism, the
conscious pleasure in sex that Lilith sought and finally found
with the lascivious demons, is a knowledge that comes to Eve
only with the world's first formal act of evil—eating the apple
—and then in the company of shame.

Who is this Eve? The weak-willed, mindlessly evil tempt-
ress and seductress of Adam, bringing about his degradation
and downfall and her own into the bargain? Or a courageous
seeker of knowledge and truth, reaching out for the symbolic
fruit as for experience and adventure? She might well have
been seeking an escape from her limitations and a resurrection
of the first Eve, the reality of her own body and experience
as opposed to the superficiality of the second Eve, real only
as seen in Adam's eyes. Could she have been yearning for the
grandeur and independence of Lilith? We are never given a
chance to find out, for Eve's very existence is merely a vehicle
for introducing shame, guilt and the toil of labor into society,
with no blame attached to man. The woman took the Fall, for
she was set up for it from the start. And with that Fall,
eroticism is conquered by guilt, and woman's sexuality is reduced to a male appendage.

The stories of Lilith and Eve are unacknowledged foun-
dation myths of woman's sexuality, and are particularly strong
in Israel, where women are still living directly within the
Jewish tradition. In Genesis, Reuben seduces Bilhah, Shchem
seduces Dinah; in Samuel, Amnon seduces Tamar, David seduces Bathsheba. Seduction or rape? It makes no difference in
the biblical view of things, for as classicists Robert Graves and
Raphael Patai note in their analysis of Hebrew myths, women
are treated "as fields to be ploughed and sown by godlike
heroes—passive, and thus necessarily guiltless if the wrong
farmer should enter. Sexual prohibitions in the Mosaic law
are addressed to men alone, and though proof of adultery
sentences the woman as well as her lover to death by stoning,

she is punished as an involuntary participant, like the luckless animal with which a man has committed bestiality."[5]

This association with bestiality—expressed in the phrase "animal desires," used by many Israeli men today to describe their sexuality—is the mainspring of the sexual strictures of the *Shulhan Aruch,* the code of Jewish law which regulates everyday behavior. The man's aim, as prescribed in the *Shulhan Aruch,* is to disassociate himself mentally as far as possible from what he is doing physically. He is urged to think of the Bible or other holy scriptures during intercourse, lest he get too caught up in it—in much the same way that when I was seriously ill as a child and had to undergo a course of penicillin injections I was urged to think of something pleasant at the moment the needle went in. At age seven I thought of roast chicken.

The model is the famous Rabbi Eliezer, of whom "it is told that he used to have cohabitation with such awe and fear that it appeared to him as if a demon was forcing him to do it."[6] Lilith, perhaps. The *Shulhan Aruch* adjures exclusive use of the "missionary position,"[7] and creates a certain confusion on technique for even the most initiated: "He should have intercourse in the most chaste possible manner; he underneath and she above him is considered unchaste; both at one and the same time is considered an improper way." Author Joseph Caro, in his little room in Safed, must have known of ways of love since lost to mankind, and unfortunately little is known of his personal life to help us solve the riddle, beyond the fact that he had "at least three wives."[8] Determined to castrate the sexual act still further by stripping it of reality, Caro ordained that "it is forbidden to glance at that place" (one understands that he means the vulva) since "by this he invokes the evil inclination upon himself. Certainly one who kisses that place violates all this, and likewise violates 'And ye shall not make your souls abominable.' "

Woman's sexuality is a threat to man's purity of soul. And yet this threat is also a duty. Although "if she [the wife] makes a verbal proposition, she exhibits a brazen shamelessness and is considered like an adulterous woman whom he must not keep," the wife is allowed to hint to her husband, by her dress and appearance, that she is in the mood for sex, in which case the husband must fulfill his marital duty. This duty is taken very seriously, for woman, unlike man in the *Shulhan Aruch*'s scheme of things, is a sexual being who must be kept reasonably satisfied so that she may be kept in her place, beneath him both physically and socially. The number of times a week or a month that a husband should fulfill this duty is stipulated according to his occupation—on the assumption that the more spiritual the occupation, the more physical strength the husband may expend in intercourse.

Nevertheless, he must be careful. Caro lists the drastic consequences—ranging from hair and teeth falling out to early death—of too much sex. He thus creates an extraordinary dilemma for the man, who is bound by divine ordinance to be fruitful and multiply with a helpmeet who threatens both soul and body. She meanwhile, forbidden on pain of divorce to verbalize her sexuality, is reduced to "feminine wiles" and to the hope that her husband be an intellectual and not a laborer.

Yet it was laborers that the young women pioneers—the *halutsot*—sought out in early twentieth-century Palestine. True, though they were laborers in practice, they were intellectuals in spirit, creating a new mysticism of labor. These idealistic forefathers and foremothers were also the reputed pioneers of Israel's putative sexual revolution—the overthrow of the sexual fears and strictures of the Jewish past for a free and proud new sexuality for men and women alike. But although on many planes their rebellion against the bourgeois norms of Eastern Europe achieved the status of a revolution, in the area of sex this rebellion remained no more than a rejection of certain aspects of traditional sexuality while it retained many of the same basic values. Thus, though the pioneers rejected the norm of marriage and therefore also the norm of virginity until marriage, they combined this revolutionary attitude with the puritanism instilled by their traditional Jewish upbringing. Freedom of choice and informality in sexual life were approved, and sexual relations were considered solely the business of those concerned, but modesty and fidelity were expected. Sexual relations, like all other social relations, were to be entered into with a "purity of heart" that was curiously innocent and basically romantic.

Esther Sturman, one of the founders of Kibbutz Merhavia in the days when it had thirty-five members, four of whom were women, described the sexual norms of her group in the third person singular—masculine form. She wrote that a member of the HaShomer pioneering movement, which founded Merhavia, "knew how to overcome desire and give up when he saw that a woman did not return his love. He did not use the woman's weakness and instability.... We were all very young, in the real spring of our days, and the spark of life burned strong in us, and more than once would it catch and burst into flame, but we always knew how to keep within limits so that we should not be consumed by the flames.... Before his eyes were the images of the fathers and mothers of the Bible. In this light he also saw the women in his environment."[9] Women were still weak and unstable and, like Eve, their sexuality was a threat and had to be kept within limits.

The scarcity of women in those early days considerably influenced such attitudes. Women were 20 to 35 percent of the total membership of the struggling new kibbutzim. They posed a threat of potentially divisive sexual competition, which was countered by an ethos of sexual asceticism, easily assimilated into early kibbutz life, which was rigorously ascetic both by necessity and by ideology. Relations between the sexes were de-eroticized and neutralized. Women, in their attempt to be equal with men, adopted male dress and behavior patterns, rejecting cosmetics, jewelry and other such bourgeois luxuries. Single men and women were often assigned sleeping quarters in large rooms that slept three or more; they were expected to, and generally did, relate to each other in a matter-of-fact and sexually neutral way. When couples nevertheless joined, they preferred to keep their relationships as quiet as possible. Attempting to be inconspicuous and discreet even when the fact of their attachment was common knowledge and fully approved by public opinion, they tried to avoid appear-

ing together in public, and when this was unavoidable, re-
frained from any overt signs of affection.[10]

Accounts such as Esther Sturman's are thus rare. Most contemporary descriptions, as writer Amos Elon observes, "read
like annals of monastic orders," with "long and rather melan-
choly platonic relationships, accompanied by the exchange of
keyed-up poems and emotional letters."[11] Such relationships
were common; one of the most famous was between the poet
Rachel Blaustein and the president-to-be of the State of Israel,
Zalman Shazar, who was later to develop a close affinity for
religious mysticism. It was a time for companionship more
than for eroticism, and for romance more than for sex, and
the sexual revolution for which it is renowned was more
an ideological resentment of the bourgeois institution of marriage than a desire for sexual equality.

Despite the absence of formal marriage, sexual relations
were taken very seriously. "The dual emphases on free love
and on restraint operated simultaneously, serving to check one
another," observed sociologist Yonina Talmon.[12] There was
almost no promiscuity and there were very few cases of shift-
ing relations: the heroine of Meyer Levin's novel about the
pioneers, *The Settlers,* who remains faithful to "her man"
long after he has left her and returned to Russia, is not as
unlikely as she might seem.[13] Sexual relations were monoga-
mous, and the rejection of marriage was merely a temporary
rejection of the symbolism of that institution, rather than of
the nuclear family.

Merhavia's Esther Sturman offers a striking example of
the dualism of sexual freedom and puritanism: "There was a
feeling of maximal freedom, but in the corner of private life
he behaved strictly and modestly. . . . He wanted to be faithful
to her and demanded purity from her. The Beduin woman,
forbidden to a stranger's touch, was his example."[14]

Sixty years later, her pride in Beduin sisterhood finds
surprising resonance in the views of Dani, a colonel in today's
Israel Defense Forces, whose blond good looks and easy self–
confidence qualify him for the slot of "typical Sabra," the new
Jew who has broken with even the physical stereotype of the

past. "We are Beduin when it comes to women," he says, with
an ease of admission that stems from a certain pride in the
fact. "Women are not really partners in sex; we use them, and
that's what they expect from us. It may not be the most ideal
way, but it deals with the problem quite well." Dani, like
most younger Israelis, is the son not of pioneers but of refugees—the hundreds of thousands who arrived in Israel just
after the State was founded. In flight from Europe's nightmare
or from Arab hostility, these people were deeply imbued with
the Jewish tradition, and their coming to Israel marked the
goal of their search for security as Jews, not for socialism or
equality. They and their children gave a sharp new twist to
the early atmosphere of innocence and abstinence in sexual
freedom. Whereas the male settlers had seen women as sexual
companions rather than sexual objects, modern Israeli men
tend to see women as means of "dealing with the problem" of
sexual desire. Sexual pragmatism has taken the place of sexual
idealism. Those "animal desires" must be satisfied; the men
assert it and the women agree.

"Listen," says Aliza, her face heavily lined at age thirty-
seven, after seven children and four abortions, "everybody
knows that men need it more than women. That's the way
they're built, so what can you do about it? You just give it to
them and that's that." From Aliza's two rooms in Jerusalem's
slum Musrara quarter to the luxury apartment of Bina in Tal-
bieh is a ten-minute walk. Though the two women represent
the poles of Israeli society—one of Oriental origin, the other
European, one poor, the other rich, one with seven children,
the other with two—their sexual opinions are astonishingly
close. "It's been proved that men have a far stronger sexual
drive than women," says Bina calmly, in a rational tone. "So
either you put yourself out a little for your man—after all,
it's not such a great sacrifice—so that you can keep him, or
you'll see him running after other women."

Aliza and Bina act as accomplices to their men in the
maintenance of Israeli's sexual status quo. And all are victims of the conspiracy they themselves perpetuate.

Women's sexuality is highly threatening to Israeli men,

as was Lilith's to Adam until she was transformed into a demoness, and as was that of the *halutsot* until it was neutralized by combining freedom with modesty and restraint.
On the one hand, the men experience desire and, nominal
heirs to the pioneers' ideology of sexual freedom, think themselves free to act on their desire. On the other, they still see
the object of that desire, women, within the value system of
the second ideology they have inherited—that of traditional
Judaism and its lore, with its disgust and fear of the woman's
body. Women's sexuality can work against the common good
unless it is kept strictly confined; and it can undermine a
man's wholeness by tempting him into bestial passion and
leading him from the path of intellectual pursuit. Modern
Israeli men have inherited both these ideologies: in the first,
public disassociation from sexuality; in the second, private
disassociation of the physical act from the spiritual being.

But the men face an additional problem. Since their
identity as Israelis is strongly linked to their identity as men,
the more they can prove themselves stereotypically masculine,
the stronger their Israeli identity becomes. The Israeli man
must prove his masculinity time and again; each proof reinforces his sense of national belonging and pride, and his rejection of any "feminine" qualities within him. His desire for
proof is nowhere more explicit than in sexual relations, where
it becomes a struggle to master female sexuality, to establish
the dominion of the male, and to block this threat to male
identity. Women are thus the means to a masculinity which requires reassurance by constant reinforcement; and quantity is
the answer to the sexual threat just as it is to the demographic
threat.

The stress on quantity means that the sexual threat is
dealt with pragmatically. "Why talk about sex?" asks Colonel
Dani rhetorically, and answers with the quips commonly used
by Israelis: "Just do it." This attitude leads to a mechani-
cal concept of sex; Israelis generally "do it" in the automatic
style one would expect of those who are counting rather
than enjoying. Men tend to measure their virility by the
number of times they can reach orgasm in one session, by

the number of women they have been with—and by the number of people who know about it. Women are the objects of their virility, counters to be collected lest self-image and reputation be threatened. Yet in so doing the men become vulnerable to betrayal of their virility.

The word "betrayal" is used regularly for extramarital affairs in Israel. Its connotations are far more drastic when a woman "betrays" her husband than vice versa, since a husband is not only allowed but even admired for extramarital affairs. A wife's affair threatens not just the security of the marriage but the man's self-image as male, virile and able to "take care of" any woman, including his wife. Betrayal, moreover, is a particularly emotion-laden word in security-conscious Israel, a word used not only for those who betray their country by spying, but also for events of national import such as Henry Kissinger's alleged betrayal of Israel in the Sinai interim agreement of 1974. Its use for a wife's extramarital affairs points up a strong link between national and sexual identity for the Israeli man.

Women are a security risk for Israeli men, in every sense of the phrase. Novelist and short-story writer Yitzhak Orpaz, who was a career officer in the Israel Defense Forces for thirteen years, expresses this risk in his continuing theme of women who undermine men's virility. His male heroes are weakened by their physical drive, which leads them to be victimized by the sexuality of women. In one story, "Horn of the Buffalo," an old man, once apparently a great hunter, climbs to a rooftop to show off his strength and dies of a stroke. In another, "The Gazelle Hunt," the woman strips and bathes in a stream, thereby distracting the attention of the man, called Adam, and depriving him of a mystic illumination that awaits him. In a third, "Little Woman," the pregnant woman literally eats the man who made her pregnant.[15] In Orpaz' world, women threaten not only identity but life itself—a betrayal of the highest order.

This female threat to the security of masculinity, fed by the Jewish tradition still lurking in the psychic background, often makes sex a joyless experience, and a stereotyped one.

The missionary position is generally the one accepted for inter-course, with little experimentation approved. Psychotherapist Naomi Abramovich noted this sexual conservatism when teaching a course on human sexuality at Tel Aviv University. "There is a kind of dual standard by which kids who claim to be rather free in their thinking have basically a rather puritanical attitude to their sexual behavior," she says. "Even those who have extramarital affairs have a very puritanical approach."

The woman who wants to be on top is seen with great ambiguity: a wild lover, perhaps, but a harlot at heart, and a patent threat to the man's superiority in her demand that this be a sexual exchange and not a monologue. Oral intercourse is generally thought of with disgust. While most men have no practical objection to fellatio, aside from a certain amount of dental anxiety, they tend to think the woman involved at the least none too nice or at the worst crazy for wanting to do such a thing. They are shocked by the suggestion of cunni-lingus: "I don't do *that!*" is a common reaction to the rare woman who attempts to take the initiative, or "That's filthy, how could you think of such a thing?" or "You don't really expect *me* to do *that.*" The more sophisticated, wised up by movies and trips abroad, say nothing and try, more in duty than in pleasure. "Oral sex is the service department of sex," says one of Tel-Aviv's avant-garde who defines himself as "a woman consumer." It humiliates the ego, which is why women are more willing to do it than men ... and for men, it raises the problem of a conflict between hygiene and spontaneity." Masturbation might be the hygienic alternative, were it not that Israelis regard it as a sick variant of the "real thing"; even on anonymous research survey forms, very few young Israeli men admit to masturbation since their first encounter with a woman, and hardly any women ever report masturbating at all.*

---

* This avoidance of the subject of masturbation reflects the religious attitude. In the *Shulhan Aruch* masturbation is strictly forbidden: it is "analogous to the killing of a person" since it is "the effusion of semen in vain." The possibility of female masturbation—logically enough in a legal code written exclusively for men—is ignored.

Humor is one way in which women deal with this situation. Since they have had little recourse but to make do, since any initiative entails the risk of the brand of whore, humor provides a kind of heavy-hearted solace. "Why are Israeli men in such a hurry in bed?" runs the standard joke among the more sexually sophisticated women. You have a choice of answers: "Because they can't wait to rush off and tell their friends all about it" or "Because they think the war's going to start any moment." Such jokes retain the self-mockery of classical Jewish humor but with an additional and particularly Israeli element of stating facts in a form defined as humorous in an attempt to laugh them off instead of dealing with them. This one zeroes in with accurate ease, for the automatic quality of the Israeli man's concept of lovemaking very often leaves women in a sexual limbo.

Many Israeli men are unaware that a woman has an orgasm, and many of those who are assume that a woman's orgasm is the automatic corollary of their own. The avantgarde Tel Avivian, who prides himself on the scope of his thinking, leafs through medical textbooks in an effort to prove that there is no such thing as a female orgasm. But the Israeli version of the "male machine"[16] is generally content to ignore the possibility.

The moot question is: to what extent do Israeli women assent in all this? A common way to deal with the problem is to deny it. Therapist Naomi Abramovich describes the elite and middle-class women's attitude toward their sexuality as being made up of "separate logic-tight compartments." Such separation avoids the conflict between the liberated myth and reality. "There's a value system based on the belief that women are equal and not exploited," says Abramovich. "And yet women are very exploited sexually. They believe they are liberated and don't need to consider sexual patterns any more, and so deny what the picture of sexual behavior really is. This kind of denial is pervasive in Israel: we are really living with a dual set of behavior, one for the country we think we would like to have, and one for the country we really have."

Paralleling this denial is plain acceptance, mainly on the

part of lower-class Oriental women. There is little doubt that the majority of older Oriental women, whose sex lives are ruled by the fear of pregnancy, are unaware of the possibility of orgasm. They assent to their definition as vessels and vassals, recipients rather than participants in the sexual act. A common answer to the question of whether they enjoy sex is a shrug or a grimace, eyebrows raised or hands outstretched, and the classic sigh followed by, "What can you do? That's how it goes, that's how it is in life." Among younger women and women of Western origin, most respond that sex is pleasurable only if they love the man they are with; but many have never experienced orgasm. "Sex feels good and warm and comforting," says Tamar, twenty-eight, married, with one child, a woman who had plenty of sexual experience before marriage but who has stayed within her marriage sexually. "I really don't miss orgasms, they don't seem to be necessary. It would be nice, I suppose, if I had them, but you get used to what you have . . ."

One could argue that a nonorgasmic sexual life might find compensation in the sense of intimacy and communion between two sexual partners, and that this increased intimacy would eventually lead to orgasm too. This might be so, were it not for the almost complete lack of any real communication about sex in Israel. The difficulties which all younger Israelis experience in communicating their feelings, rooted in their view of emotion as weakness and covered over by the "Don't talk about it, just do it" philosophy, makes sexual communication all but impossible. Unable to verbalize what they feel or want, Israeli women resign themselves to the male view of sex, a resignation made easy by the almost total lack of sex education in the country.

Sex education has always been a particularly sensitive subject in Israel, one that threatened the uneasy stand-off between the theopolitic—the political power of the religious establishment—and the secular politic which ruled the Ministry of Education. The very idea of confrontation between the two confounded any move to initiate a proper sex education program throughout the country's highly centralized school system. But when the National Religious Party gained control of the Education Ministry after the May 1977 elections, as part of its coalition agreement with Menahem Begin's Likud government, the prospects for sex education, never high, plummeted. The NRP may not go so far as to order that the *Shulhan Aruch* be taught as a sex manual in the schools. But it is expected to exercise tight control over existing experimental programs.

In the early seventies, a Unit for Family Life was quietly set up within the Education Ministry, its title reflecting the attitude of the majority of those involved with the subject. The Unit took a passive stance, adopting a policy of advising schools or teachers who asked for help rather than taking the initiative. "The fear of what the religious will do or think has multiplied since 1948," says Dr. Moshe Lancet, a gynecologist who is one of the Unit's advisers and who has written two books for adolescents which mercifully do not link sex exclusively with marriage. In recent years, however, more teachers turned to the Unit, which started training a cadre of teachers intellectually and emotionally equipped to handle sex education. But the Unit's future under NRP administration is now unclear, and no one knows to what extent the few trained teachers will be able to continue their work.

At present, even the most elementary sex education is available only to the minority of Israeli youth, and then generally in cursory and superficial form. The one lecture sometimes given, if any is given at all, may cover the essentials of reproduction, contraception and VD, but there is no education for sexual life. An idea of what is typically offered is the bemused tale of a girl in one of Jerusalem's elite high schools: "This huge fat man with a stick, nearly bald, came in one day with a chart and talked for an hour about the physiology of the reproductive system and the dangers of VD. And that was the last we saw of him."

Some sex educators relax in the knowledge that girl recruits in the army receive sex education as part of their basic training. They ignore the fact that only half the population of eighteen-year-old girls in the country is recruited into the army, and that the army's form of sex education is a two-hour lecture given to a platoon of two hundred recruits, each one far too shy to ask questions in front of a hundred and ninety-nine others. The content of the lecture is physiology, contraception and VD, and those who have already been exposed to such a lecture at school nod off to sleep. Those for whom this information is almost entirely new emerge confused by the sudden barrage of data. Unable to absorb so much at once, they reject most of it, remembering only odd details that fit into their own systems of rumor and old wives' tales. The lecture takes no account whatsoever of the strong sexual pressures to which the girls will be subjected in the army. "With whom and when you have intercourse is your decision; I won't talk about that," declares the army lecturer at the start of his talk, dismissing the question uppermost in the minds of most of his audience.

The army passes the buck by saying that the schools should see to sex education, and that the only reason it gives anything at all is because it knows the schools often do not. The schools pass the buck by referring to the pressure of the theopolitic and arguing that they cannot give instruction of which parents would not approve. Parents pass the buck by arguing that the schools are better equipped to give sex education than they are.

The buck has gathered moss in all this passing. A 1974 survey of high schoolers by a team headed by Moshe Lancet[17] revealed a very low level of knowledge about even the rudiments of sex, with girls consistently scoring lower than boys. On a scale of 1 to 7 on knowledge of anatomy the highest-scoring group of students—sixteen- to seventeen-year-old boys —scored an average of 1.9. Nevertheless, 41 percent of the boys in this group were sexually experienced. (Lancet was attacked by delegations of prim high schoolers after publishing his report, not for his findings on sexual ignorance, but for his statistics on the number of those who had started having intercourse. The high schoolers claimed that the actual numbers were far lower and that his findings sullied their good name and were libelous.) The behavior of the girls was still more inconsistent: by age sixteen or seventeen, 16 percent reported that they had had sexual intercourse, two thirds of them using no contraception. Lancet's comment that "the low incidence of pregnancies is probably due to the good care of the God of Israel" would be funny if it were not so sad. In fact pregnancies are probably as frequent as one would expect, but are terminated by abortion. The low percentage of girls reporting intercourse as compared to boys has led some critics of Lancet's research to argue that the girls are underreporting. This could very well be true, since even when their anonymity is guaranteed, many girls find it hard to come to terms with the discrepancy between what they do and what they feel about it.

Dr. Helen Antonovsky, a member of Lancet's original research team, followed up indications of dissonance in the behavior of some of the sexually experienced girls.[18] Thirty percent of those who do report intercourse, for example, say that it is important for a girl to be a virgin at marriage. Many report having been pressured into intercourse rather than choosing it, and their sexual experience is either highly ambivalent or simply negative. A disproportionate number of the "discrepant" girls, Antonovsky found, were of Oriental origin—more than twice as many as those of Western origin. Despite the fact that they do not approve of what they do, girls who have had intercourse once are likely to continue, apparently on the reasoning that since virginity cannot be regained, nothing remains to be lost.

These girls are stranded in the mire of contradictions between Oriental and modern standards, and within the modern standard itself. They attempt to imitate what they see as the sophistication of the modern middle class, unaware that their imitation is no more than a cruel farce, since the apparently open middle-class sexual mores cover up a basic sexual attitude that is little in advance of the Oriental one. Sexual exploitation is hidden under a veneer of sophistication in the largely Ashkenazi middle class, while it is explicit in the mainly Oriental lower class, where the men subscribe to the Levantine view of women as property, cooks and child-bearers.

These men cling to the stereotype of the "masculine" Israeli as a means of identification with a society in which they are on the fringe despite their numerical strength. The Oriental daughters, caught between the traditional values of virginity and female ignorance that prevail at home and the superficial sexual freedom which they see in the middle class, attempt to copy the middle-class norm of behavior while clinging to traditional attitudes. This severe contradiction in self-concept can radically affect their lives.

For a small number it is a major factor leading to prostitution. Once she has lost her virginity, aware that she is regarded as "no better than a whore" by her family and immediate society, a young Oriental woman may well resign herself to her fate and adapt her behavior to her self-image by actually becoming a prostitute. Studies of Israel's 2,000 or so full-time prostitutes (some estimates put the number at close to six thousand including "moonlighters"[19]), nearly all of whom are Oriental in origin, demonstrate how a young girl living in a city slum neighborhood can be singled out by local racketeers for prostitution.[20] A well-thought-out system is put into operation: seduction and then enticement into prostitution on the grounds that the girl is already completely dishonored and might as well cut her losses by making use of that dishonor. Such girls generally come from particularly difficult or strict home environments. The gangsters know they will have no recourse other than to give in, for once they are or are even rumored to be no longer virgins, they will be cut off from their families.

While the vast majority of young Oriental women avoid the trap of prostitution, many fall into another trap by converting the inconsistency in their self-concept into hysterical symptoms. "In all the years I worked in the States," says therapist Abramovich, who immigrated to Israel in 1972, "I never saw so many hysterical symptoms—headaches and so on —as I've seen here. They're very much related to sexual frigidity, and are close to the old-fashioned hysteria that Freud described, a hysteria that you usually see in people who've had a very Victorian upbringing."

In true Victorian style, young Oriental women endeavor to maintain their virginity until marriage, but it is a task fraught with anxieties. Orna, for example, is just eighteen and comes from a family of nine. Her mother arrived in Israel in 1951, from Iraq, and her father shortly thereafter, from Morocco. Her father left home in 1970, leaving the family to live mainly on welfare, but returns now and then, blind drunk, to beat both wife and children. Occasionally he swears everlasting love, occasionally he threatens their lives. She is still haunted by her father's attempt to rape her, at age eleven, which she resisted, and by her mother's silence and passivity when she found out about it. Orna, the eldest child, was determined not to fall into the same vicious cycle of suffering as her mother, and this gave her the grit and concentration to finish high school and be accepted into the army, both very unusual for a girl from her background. Under great social pressure from her friends to start sexual relations—"All my girl friends have already started and think I'm really childish about it"—she was persuaded that indeed there was little point in waiting until she married. But she decided that she would maintain her virginity until she met someone she felt she really loved, which happened shortly after her eighteenth birthday. After much insistence, she assented to go to bed with him. "I decided that here was someone I could trust, and whom I loved, and whom I wanted—he just had to touch me to get me excited—and so when I felt that it would be right, I said yes. Then he didn't want me . . ." Orna had innocently taken the decision that turned her from idealized and unattainable virgin into whore. Her boyfriend, eight years older than she, could not come to terms with her real sexuality. He was also afraid of intercourse, since he realized how big a step it was for her and wanted to avoid too deep an emotional involvement. The relationship ended in miserable sordidness when she became pregnant—he had ejaculated against her hymen during heavy petting—and lost her virginity in an illegal abortion: a sad ending to what she had hoped would be a joyful experience.

Tirza, also eighteen, comes from a poor but relatively

well educated Algerian family. She dressed and made up with sophistication while she worked tentatively at this and that job and searched around for the right man to take her out of the slum and realize her dream of ascending the social ladder. She finally picked one, reliable and hardworking, and put him through a series of tests to make sure he really was as solid as he seemed. She ticked off the points on her fingers two weeks before the wedding: "He doesn't play cards, he doesn't smoke hashish, he doesn't raise a finger in anger—I know because I've made him angry on purpose to see what he'd do. He wouldn't even go to bed with me before the wedding because he respects my virginity—I suggested it even, just to make sure. Of course I would have said no if he'd said yes, but no, he was fine." The couple spent the wedding night in her parents' house, and she could not sleep; she continued not sleeping and started behaving strangely, until the signs of schizophrenia were so unmistakable that her parents took her to a mental hospital. She still cannot talk about what it was that triggered her breakdown, but there is little doubt that it was the shock of the wedding night that took her over the edge. At eighteen Tirza is still shakily trying to come to terms with her experience, and is pregnant from that first night.

At sixteen, Iris, one of a large Iraqi family making its way up in life, was not a particularly bright student, but high school was important for her, since it was a step toward realizing her aspirations for a better life than her mother's. She had been trying hard. For four months, however, her work has been going downhill; she had been morose and silent in class and outside it, and sometimes she simply stayed away for a day or two with vague excuses of illness. Talking to her about what was happening was difficult; she would not respond. And then one day she broke into tears. Four months previously, she sobbed out, she had been raped by a stranger, at midnight, just fifty yards from her home. I was the first person she had told about it. She had not dared tell her parents, afraid that they would brand her a prostitute for losing her virginity and turn her out of the house, or at the least accuse her of provoking the rape and try to marry her off immediately, to cover up the dishonor, meanwhile keeping her locked up at home. She had not told her friends, since she was afraid of their reaction: they would talk and joke about it, and then all her acquaintances would know. And of course she had not gone to the police. She had spent the last four months in deep depression over the loss of her virginity, which disturbed her as much as the rape itself, and how this would influence her chances for marriage and her relationship with her boyfriend if he ever found out she was not still a virgin.

While the outcomes of two of these three stories—Orna's virgin pregnancy and Tirza's madness—are clearly exceptional, the dynamics of all three give an accurate reflection of the way young Oriental women handle the superficially liberal but basically reactionary dual sexual standard.

The stress on virginity is strongest among Oriental Israelis but is by no means limited to them. Sociologist Rivka Bar-Yosef found that 60 percent of Tel Aviv women—aged twenty to forty, mainly middle-class, and with somewhat more Western- than Oriental-origin women—opposed premarital sex, the majority of them on the grounds that it is detrimental to successful marriage.[21] Only 20 percent of the women had had premarital sex themselves. Higher education lessens the emphasis placed on virginity. Few of the Tel Aviv women had been to college, and indeed Bar-Yosef found a more permissive approach among Hebrew University students, only 14 percent of whom opposed premarital sex. But approval was still within limits: 50 percent argued that premarital sex was permissible only if the couple concerned were in love, and a further 13 percent only if the couple were engaged to be married;[22] 60 percent of the women students believed that sex could only be satisfactory within the framework of a love relationship.

What happened to the "swinging Israel" of international repute, surveyed in such hopeful pieces as *Playboy*'s 1970 report[23] on "the land of milk and honeys"? That article, confused by the "thorough unpredictability" of the chances of getting an Israeli woman into bed, wisely resolved the problem by concentrating instead on where to dine. Its confusion was ironic, for like *Playboy*, Israeli women are attractiveness-oriented rather than sex-oriented, concerned with the status and wrappings of sex rather than with sexual experience itself.

These are the Eve Twos, whose flesh and blood is carefully covered over for the sake of appealing to modern Adams demanding supremacy. According to one of Israel's leading cosmeticians, Judith Muller, whose perfume company produces a range of scents all named after Biblical characters, Israel boasts more qualified cosmeticians per capita than any other country in the world, all of them gainfully employed. It also has one of the highest bra consumption rates in the world. While the Israel Defense Forces provide only the most cursory form of sex education for female recruits, they provide countless hours of cosmetics advice and demonstrations, given by cosmetics companies who volunteer their time "for the army." The army sees no contradiction in the fact that it offers discount cosmetics in army stores but not contraceptives, thus helping women soldiers to be sexually attractive but not sexually free.

Women exist sexually for men, not for themselves. According to journalist Tamar Meroz, they should go to a sexologist to get themselves straightened out if they feel they are being treated as sexual objects. She quotes one sexologist, unfortunately unnamed: "A wife should be like a mistress, not think of her own pleasure but just of his, so that he will be happy and feel masculine and strong; she should use any means she can think of just to give him this feeling."[24] Ilana, a brightly dyed blond mother of three who works as a shop assistant in the mornings, agrees. "My husband comes home late, about eight in the evening, so that gives me time to get everything right—the kids quietly in bed, my face properly made up, pretty clothes on, the place clean, everything ready for him. He should always see me attractive so that he'll never lose interest in me. And the one rule that's most important is never to refuse him, no matter how you feel. Unless I want him running after other women, that's my task, to keep him close because he gets all he wants that way. As long as he thinks

I'm attractive to other men, he'll want me and be proud of me, and won't go running off for fear that I might."

The object is to be a sexual object, since this is the means of gaining the end of security. It may be the security of a firmly feminine sex role, or that of a house, children and a husband to support the woman. The two, in fact, are complementary. Journalist Andrew Meisels neatly picked up the ethics of Israeli women's sexuality in his novel *Six Other Days*. His heroine says, "You see, Oded, we women really have no morals at all. It's you men who created morality in the first place, and we just follow along as your philosophy twists and turns from one generation to the next. You want girls to be chaste till marriage? We will be chaste till marriage. ... You want girls to be lovers first and wives afterward? We will make love to you first and marry you later. What you men call morality doesn't matter in the slightest to us. What we have all wanted since Eve was love and a family—and the precise road we take to that end is totally immaterial to us."[25]

The problem is that making love first and marrying later can be a risky proposition for a woman, a risk with which many single women, whether never married, divorced or widowed, are well acquainted. Israel is a society of gossip and rumor, a small community in which "everybody knows everybody," or at least so it seems. And since part of the man's sense of masculinity comes from recounting his sexual exploits to his friends, the woman runs the risk of having her sex life dissected in cafés and at parties by people with whom she is barely or not at all acquainted. Once the question "Does she give?" is answered positively, the assumption is that it is positive for all. And some women, feeling honor-bound to their own dishonor, as it were, also assume that a body once given should be given again, no matter to whom. "If she can't give herself to whom she chooses, let everybody have her" is how one character describes the promiscuity of another in Yael Dayan's novel *Dust*.[26]

The groupiness of Israeli life, understandably strong in a society searching for a national norm and using smaller groups to help establish this, allows little privacy. Gossip is so openly parlayed that rumors often become more real than reality, even for those who figure in them. It is almost as if no act or event is real unless known and discussed, whether by the group of friends (the *hevra*), the school class, the family group, the neighborhood, or even the national group. And this holds true for sex as much as for any other activity. One often has the impression that what happens between two people within four walls is irrelevant compared with what people outside those walls imagine is happening. While Freudians maintain that there are four people in a bed every time a couple make love—the couple, his mother and her father—in Israel there are dozens if not hundreds of people: the immediate *hevra* and the extended *hevra* groups linked to the original one through gossip.

Miriam, a rebellious unmarried production assistant at Israel Television, a hotbed of sexual and other intrigue, finds the gossip insufferable: "I just have to walk out of the building with a guy and everyone assumes we're already in bed. And as if that weren't bad enough, the minute we're alone he comes on with, 'Everyone thinks we're doing it, so we might as well, come on, you've got nothing to lose...'" The line works more often than not: a shrug of the shoulders, a hop into bed, another notch for the man's belt, another fleeting moment of illusory closeness for the woman. Muses Miriam sadly, "Israelis are too close to be intimate."

They are too close in every way. They live on top of one another, physically and metaphorically. Crammed into shoddily built apartment blocks, they hear each other flush the toilets. Seated on hard-backed chairs around the coffee table on a Friday night, they hear the details of each others' "private" lives, tales of sexual adventurism whose very stereotypy makes them surrealistically sexless. What Israelis rarely grasp is the distinction between eros and sex that Rollo May makes in *Love and Will*—the distinction between "manipulating organs" and making love, between sexual stereotypy and sexual experience. "Sex is a need," says May, "but eros is a desire.... It can be agreed that the aim of the sex act in its zoological and physiological sense is indeed the orgasm. But the aim of eros is not: eros seeks union with the other person in delight and passion, and the procreating of new dimensions of experience which broaden and deepen the being of both persons."[27]

The intimacy and communication of eros is hard to find in Israel, where so much emphasis is placed on quantity, and the sexual experience itself is often such a one-sided affair. Sex is a measure of virility and of national identity for the man, and for the woman a means to security. In the search for security and the concern with appearances, Israeli men and women have created a sexual anomie; they use sex, but they often miss out on much of its joy and beauty. Secure in home and marriage, the Israeli wife feels strong enough in her sense of belonging to smile condescendingly in maternal forgiveness of her husband's prodigal ways with other women. Married women seek out extramarital affairs far less often than married men; they do not need reassurance of their femininity in the sexual sense since they have it in their everyday roles as wife and mother. The payoff of sex takes different forms for men and women, but it is essentially the same: security of identity in a country beset by insecurity.

6

The Sword and
the Plowshare

The Israel Defense Forces (I.D.F.) and the kibbutz are probably the two most famous images of Israel. They symbolize the duality and simultaneity of life and death—sword and plowshare. And they are the stars in the firmament of the myth of Israeli women's liberation, beckoning to legions of hopeful admirers including such eminent feminists as Betty Friedan and Simone de Beauvoir.[1] But the stars are evanescent, fading on close inspection to a reality in direct confrontation with the image. Though their afterglow lingers on, both the army and the kibbutz are prime examples not of the liberation of Israeli women, but of their imposed and accepted regression into the feminine stereotype. Both institutions reinforce rather than dispel the biological and "real woman" myths.

The year 1973 was the last chance for photographers to catch that rousing image of Israeli women soldiers marching, Uzi submachine gun on shoulder, in smart formation through the streets of Jerusalem, for this was to be the last of the big military Independence Day parades. Crowds lining the streets gave as much applause to the women's units as to the elite paratroop units. Tanned, miniskirted and beautiful, some smiling and others locked into serious concentration, the marching women aroused a paternal pride in the crowds, as well as a none-too-paternal appreciation.

Today, women recruits march just as smartly in passing-out parades after basic training. And that is generally the last time they carry a gun in the army. For Israel's army women are wearing paper khaki. They are the secretaries, the clerks, the telephonists, the teletypists, the nurses, the teachers and the social workers of the I.D.F.—filling all the service roles determined by the feminine stereotype. They are specifically forbidden to enter combat or to hold any post that might bring them into or near combat.

In all three arms of the United States Army, 571 out of a total of 628 job classifications are open to women.[2] I.D.F. women, however, have the choice of only some 150 jobs (out of a total not publishable for security reasons, but certainly close to that of the American army). While women serve as helicopter pilots, transport pilots, jet pilots, test pilots and astronauts in the American air force, Israeli women are disqualified from serving or even training as pilots in the Israeli air force. While women in the American navy serve on board ship, Israeli women are generally kept strictly ashore. And while half of the women inducted into the American air force in 1975 were trained as technicians and engineers, Israel has a mere handful of women airplane technicians. There are six women generals in the United States Army, and even in a country generally regarded as somewhat backward in women's rights —France—there is one. In Israel there are none, and the highest rank accorded a woman is that of colonel. While the United States trains its women officers alongside men, Israel has separate officers' training for women, for the good reason that the content of that training has little in common with that given men.

And yet Israel is the only country in the world that has compulsory recruitment for women. The reason is a dire need for manpower in the I.D.F., an army on constant military alert and in all-too-frequent combat. Women do not serve alongside men: they replace men in jobs considered within women's capacity, so that the men are released for frontline service. The I.D.F. women quickly learn that their job is service, running the back rooms so that the men are free for combat. Psychologist Tamar Breznitz-Svidovsky, who has studied women's reactions in wartime, sums up women's role in the I.D.F. and its implications with the statement that "women come out of the army more inclined to the feminine stereotype than when they go in."

"The army would fall apart if not for the girls," says a senior Women's Corps officer, clearly delighted with the idea of being the power behind the throne. She is right. The Women's Corps runs the basic services of the army's infrastructure—the clerical, switchboard and social services without which the vast task of administering an active army would become hopelessly entangled. But apart from these services, its scope is severely limited.

Two job classifications are reserved solely for women. One is typing. The other is parachute folding.

Three types of jobs are entirely closed to women. The first type is the job involving physical strain. Among these is truck driving. Despite the fact that British A.T.S. women drove heavy trucks in the Cairo-Jerusalem run during the Second World War, and that women truck drivers regularly make the coast-to-coast run in the United States, Israeli army women drive generals, not trucks. The commanding officer of Women's Corps, Dalia Raz, is pragmatic and somewhat resigned about it. "The social norm in Israel today," she says, "is that women don't drive heavy vehicles. I'd like to see the reactions of the women soldiers, the mothers and the public if I made them drive trucks. And even if a girl could drive a truck, where would she drive it in wartime? To the front. And we don't send girls to the front in wartime."[3]

The second type of job closed to women is that which "because of environmental or service conditions" is not considered suitable for women. Women do not serve as pump attendants in army gas stations, for instance, and they do not serve in places where there are no showers available. The third type closed to women is any job that will bring them into contact with combat.

In the event of war, any women who are at the front lines—for example, as company clerks—are immediately transported to the rear. The reasons for keeping women out of combat are legion. One is the extreme sensitivity in Israel to women casualties. Sensitivity to all casualties is high, but if a woman is involved, public and army morale plummets. While it is accepted that a man may die or be injured for his country, a female casualty touches the major nerve of paternal protectiveness toward women. The army exists to protect Israel's women, not to endanger them in its ranks.

Another reason is the one most often quoted by army sources: torture and rape. "No mother in Israel, nor I," says C.O. Raz, "would want to see a girl soldier a prisoner in the hands of the Syrians." Their fate would indeed be horrible, as Israeli experience in the 1948 War of Independence proved, and as that of male P.O.W.s in Syrian jails (which included rape and random sadism) indicates; but whether it would be any more horrible than the men's experience cannot be assessed. Is this fear of rape, which reaches the dimensions of what one sociologist calls a "rape fetish," really the main reason for keeping women out of combat posts? Or is it a rationalization of another reason often intimated by senior officers—the cult of fertility and the underlying biological myth?

Senior I.D.F. officers, both female and male, almost invariably argue that the army's function is to fight, and that therefore, as one senior woman officer explains, "From the very nature of the army, you can't have equality of the sexes in it. A woman's just not built for fighting, physically or mentally. Her aspirations lie in another direction altogether —marrying and having children. . . . I know women were fighting in 1948 during the War of Independence, and I'm very glad it's changed. I don't think women should fight, not because they're soft, but because their purpose in life is to tend to the next generation."

The disturbing implication that men *are* built to fight is reiterated by right-wing Member of Knesset Geula Cohen, an underground fighter in the years prior to 1948. "The army is not the natural place for a woman as God created her," states

Cohen, leaving one with the conclusion that it is the natural place for men. "The Israeli woman is an organic part of the family of the people of Israel," she continues, "and the woman soldier is the practical symbol of this. But she is a woman of Israel and a mother of Israel, and it is natural that after regular service her reserve service take the form of being the wife of a soldier, the mother of a soldier, the sister of a soldier, and the grandmother of a soldier."[4]

One of the few voices raised in dissent is that of one of the toughest generals in the I.D.F. Rafael Eytan (Raful), head of Northern Command, is a grizzled and brilliant veteran who knows the value of life as such, whether male or female. Thus he is capable of asking such questions, say his associates, as "Why can't women drive tanks?" or, "Why is it any harder to tell parents that their daughter has died in combat than to tell them about their son?" But on this issue Raful is a loner on the Central Staff; his attitude is interpreted as just another expression of his toughness, and on this point he is ignored.

The vast majority of Israeli women, and of army women, would not support him. In a survey by psychologist Tamar Breznitz-Svidovsky, close to 90 percent maintained that women should not serve in combat units. The reasons given most frequently: "Women scare too easily," "Women are too weak," "Women should wait at home for their husbands."[5]

It is in the context of this last comment that yet another reason for keeping women out of combat turns up: the practical reason of familism. "You don't even need to go into the whole question of mental and physical ability," argues C.O. Dalia Raz. "The simple fact is that in wartime the whole country is organized for the men to be out fighting. How can I call a married woman with children into reserve service when her husband's already been called up and she's looking after the children, which is absolutely legitimate? No doubt there would be some women soldiers ready, out of adventurism rather than sense, to volunteer as tank drivers, for instance, but after their regular service they'd get married and have children and then I can't call them up for the reserves,

so we'd only have half a tank unit to send into battle." The
I.D.F. thus accepts the definition of a woman's role based on
children and home, and a man's role based on activities outside the home. When there is no war, fathers could care for
the children in the same way mothers do when the fathers
are called into reserve service; in wartime, communal child-
care facilities could be established. But neither of these possibilities is at all realistic within the framework of present
sex roles in Israel. And both would require new and un-
popular legislation.

At present, the law forbids Dalia Raz to call married
women into reserve service even if she wanted to. The Defense
Service Act states that men can be called into the reserves—
the main force of Israel's largely citizens' army—up to age
fifty-six, and women up to age thirty-six. But married women
and mothers are exempted, and in fact very few of those
single women eligible for reserve service are ever called on, to
the great relief of most and the bitter frustration of a few.

The reserve service limitations develop from the limitations on women in regular service. The Defense Service Act
states that any woman who is married and/or pregnant or a
mother cannot be recruited into the I.D.F. Thus, up to 8
percent a year of eighteen-year-old Israeli women, those who
marry early, do not serve in the army, since in law their duties
to their husbands are considered more important than their
duties to the State. An ironic comment on this is the inter-
pretation given to the acronym Zahal (*Zva Hagana Le'Israel*—
Israel Defense Forces) which is scrawled over the wall of one
of the lecture rooms in *Bahad 12,* the main training camp for
women recruits. There Zahal stands for *Zrichot Hayinu
Lehithaten!*—"We should have gotten married!"

A further 17 to 18 percent of women are released from
army service on religious grounds, again according to law.
This is the result of another compromise with the religious
political parties, who were opposed from the start to women
serving in the army, arguing that army service will lead to
their moral disintegration. Each year religious pressure groups
go so far as to send a special pamphlet to all eighteen-year-old

women advising them on what to say to the recruitment board in order to escape army service on the grounds that they are religious, whether they are or not. These groups probably receive the names from the population registry of the Ministry of the Interior, which is controlled by the National Religious Party. In June 1977 their task was made easier. As part of its coalition agreement with the ultra-Orthodox Agudath Israel party, Menahem Begin's new Likud government stipulated that henceforth women declaring themselves religious to avoid army service need offer no proof of the sincerity of their faith.

A further 2 percent or so do not serve in the army for reasons of health. But by far the most disturbing exemption from regular army service is the 25 percent or so, nearly all Israeli-born and of Oriental origin, who "do not have basic qualifications" and are therefore rejected. These are women who cannot read or write fluently, or whose problems (low attention span, low threshold of patience, inability to tolerate discipline) stem in part from their poor schooling up to the compulsory age of fourteen, when most of them leave school formally (though in practice many have dropped out before then). Educational requirements are higher for women, since they do mainly clerical work. If they were men, nearly all this 25 percent would be absorbed into the army; but where the army is willing to take in and educate illiterate men, it is not willing to do the same for women. Many of the 25 percent are all too pleased to escape what they consider two wasted years out of their lives, but just as many suffer from the stigma of rejection, and see their ineligibility as both a punishment and a judgment of their worth in society.

The result is that only about half of eighteen-year-old Israeli women serve in the army. In 1975 the number was the highest in many years—51 percent. The fact that those who do serve do so for only two years (men for three), and are then unlikely to serve in the reserves, is used to justify their service role within the army. The argument is often presented in economic terms: the amount of time it would take to train a woman for a skilled job in the army—as a pilot, for example —would not be justified by the amount of time she would actually serve. While a man's service can total nearly nine years—three years in the regular army followed by up to two months' reserve service each year for thirty-five years—a woman generally serves only her two regular years. Thus the army does not get the requisite payoff for its investment in training—a valid argument if one agrees that family should take priority over country for women but not for men.

Few army women question their situation, and a tough time awaits those who do. When one woman in a round-table discussion at a command army camp said that she felt limited as a secretary and wanted to "get out" into a more responsible job, she was accused of being what the other women called "egoistic," of putting her own feelings above national duty. The Women's Corps officer suggested that she start a gymnastics class as a means of working off her frustration. To all the others the situation seemed quite right and natural: "You can hardly expect men to do what we do," said Ofra, a telephonist. "They'd just be no good at it, they wouldn't have the patience, they'd go to pieces in our jobs. And besides, how can you imagine a man typing? We don't want to do what the men do, and we don't want them to do what we do. We want to be women, not men."

The I.D.F. agrees. In basic training (three weeks for women, three months for men), women are taught to handle two weapons: the Kalachnikov rifle, and the Uzi submachine gun. And yet, except on *Nahal* (agricultural border settlements established by the army), they never use this training, not even in target practice. Why then are they taught to shoot at all? The official explanation, from an army pamphlet, is that "a woman must learn to use various types of light weapons so as to be able to operate them in case of need, even if only in self-defense."[6] This translates into the "last-ditch defense" theory put forward by senior army officers who argue, with many interjections in the vein of "it should never come to that," that if a war situation becomes very desperate, women too can lift arms in defense of their country, or at least of themselves. Retorts Women's Corps C.O. Dalia Raz: "Absolutely not. In three weeks I should make a fighter out of a woman? That's not the aim of the basic training course. For them to be fighters they'd need proper training, and knowing how to use two guns is not proper training. They're not taught tactics, for instance. . . . The aim of teaching them how to use a gun is to give them the feeling that they're in the army, of being a soldier." In other words, it is good for morale.

In addition to the thirty-five hours spent learning how to hold, clean, assemble and fire a gun (each woman actually fires five rifle bullets and twenty-five submachine-gun bullets), women recruits also learn unarmed combat, again, according to the official explanation, for self-defense. But it is intended for self-defense against compatriot would-be rapists rather than enemy ones. The twelve hours of mixed judo and karate basics are not intended to teach judo and karate, which Raz well knows is impossible in so short a time, but "to give them a bit of self-confidence." It is needed. After the rape and murder of a woman soldier hitchhiking back to base after a leave in 1974, the army upped self-defense lessons for women recruits from four hours to twelve, in the hope that the extra touch of self-confidence might help prevent such attacks.

Feminist Miriam Tzur states matters more bluntly than Dalia Raz: "Basic training was a farce; we barely learned how to fire a gun. In officers' training all we got were lectures on Zionism and patriotism. I don't mean to imply that this isn't important. But if women can finish officers' training with no basic military knowledge, it's a scandal. . . . The army treats women soldiers as if they were little children who manage to carry a glass into the kitchen without breaking it. Any small achievement is magnified out of proportion, while real opportunities for achievement are limited."[7]

Photographs of women parachutists in the army might seem to indicate otherwise, but in fact the only job for women in the paratroop corps is folding parachutes—a boring but high-status job for women, since it brings them into contact with the elite paratroopers. Folders are allowed to take a jumping course, however. Raz explains: "It gives them a sense of how important the work is. But it's just a course, that's all —the girl doesn't use it, she would never do it in battle, it's not her job in the army. It's a kind of privilege." Another morale booster.

Although the army boosts the morale of its women by such means as teaching them how to fire a gun and awarding privileges such as learning how to parachute, it generally regards the women themselves as means of boosting the morale of the men. While Raz is sophisticated enough to play this down, stressing instead the importance of the work that women do in the I.D.F., her predecessors, military commentators, and senior army personnel have always stressed the morale-building aspect of women's army service. Ruth Muscal, who was pressured into resigning as C.O. of the Women's Corps in 1975 because she was pregnant, emphasized that women, "by the fact of their presence, raise the morale of their unit" and "add a qualitative dimension to the I.D.F." She noted that the acronym of the Hebrew for Women's Corps, *Chen,* means "charm," and that it could also stand for *chochma nisteret*—the hidden wisdom "which every woman has by her nature, and indeed is required to use in the army, contributing to its social quality."[8] Military commentators Edward Luttwak and Dan Horowitz explain this social quality by stating that "the presence of women in the army has reduced the vulgarity and free-floating violence so frequent in all-male armies,"[9] a fact attributable as much to the heavy reliance of the I.D.F. on civilian reserves and to its service on home ground as to the presence of women.

Army women, however, are proud of their much-vaunted contribution to morale. "My job is to spoil the soldiers," said Shoshi, a company clerk, when she received a commendation for outstanding service. "How do I spoil them? I bring them sandwiches and coffee to their positions in the middle of the night, see to it that the letters and parcels from home get to them every day, and so on."[10] This, in addition to the typing and clerical work of the company, is the unwritten duty of the company clerk—who is immediately trucked back to home base, leaving the soldiers without sandwiches and coffee, during a high alert or war.

A snide report by newspaper columnist Gideon Lev en-

larged on the extent of this spoiling. Describing how moving
it was to arrive at his post for reserve service and see the
women soldiers stationed there sad at the departure of the last
bunch of reservists, he noted in particular "one snub-nosed
girl crying on the shoulder of one of the reserve officers." A
month later, at the end of his unit's service, he saw the scene
repeated, with the same girl crying again, but this time on
the shoulder of one of Lev's officers.[11]

What Lev was getting at is a phenomenon which causes
great unease in the army spokesman's office when it is broached:
the sexual mores within the I.D.F. While the spokesman's
office willingly approves photographs of women soldiers
tending to their makeup amidst the sands of Sinai, on the
premise that such photos are good for morale, it is hyper-
sensitive to any follow-up on this sexual attractiveness. Journalist Ada Saar created a minor furor in Central Command
and the Spokesman's Office when she wrote one of the few
articles ever published in Israel on the subject. "During their
army service," said the final version of her story, "women are
subjected to sexual pressures, temptations and tensions, and
certainly need a strong backbone to be able to realize what
they really want and what they are not interested in, to withstand the atmosphere of 'what difference does it make?' "[12]

This atmosphere is very often the pervasive one, encouraged by the special and public privileges accorded their girl
friends by some senior officers in the army, and by such current jokes as the one about a camp commander in Sinai who
is rumored to have bedded not a single one of the women
soldiers serving under him.

However crude and exaggerated, such jokes point up the
fact of sexual exploitation of women in the army, which is
rare in the explicit "either you do, or . . ." form, but is quite
common in a subtler and more socially approved version.
Many women soldiers provide sexual as well as social and
administrative services—a natural phenomenon, perhaps, in
a mixed army, but one degraded by the atmosphere in which
it takes place. Women soldiers who refuse to sleep with officers
and soldiers earn themselves the nicknames "iceberg" or

"nun": "It was either be a mattress or be a nun," says one attractive army graduate, bitterly. But few women take sex in the army so seriously. Most dismiss it with the Israeli shrug and raised eyebrows, and a "Why not?" or "What's the difference?"

Although not openly approved, such an attitude is not exactly frowned upon. Israel's top military correspondent, Zeev Schiff, writes in what is apparently a semi-official history of the I.D.F. that "Entering the army at age 18, for most young women, means their first experience away from home and their introduction to sexual intercourse. . . . The easygoing familiarity promotes an eroticism that is matter-of-fact and controlled."[13] Schiff may have been thinking of the nickname for the basic training camp for women: Combat Camp. Why? "Because that's where the first blood is spilled." Though such vulgar jokes may not reflect the norm, their existence encourages the buildup of strong sexual pressures which easily lead to sexual exploitation.

Not only does the army give women no means of dealing with these pressures, but it also specifically punishes those who get pregnant as a result of ignorance and the inability to say no. Any woman who gets pregnant during her two-year service is immediately discharged, even if she has already had an abortion. Pregnant women are forbidden to serve in the army, and in extraordinary obeisance to the letter of the law, the army applies this rule to women who have been pregnant in the past, even if the pregnancy was terminated by abortion. It has justified this ruling by arguing that since abortions were illegal, it could not overlook a woman's having one. But by mid-1977, it had still not announced whether it would change the rules to accommodate the abortion law reform passed earlier in the year, which should allow legal abortion for single women. The discharge ruling is highly discriminatory in practice. Women who can raise the money or who have understanding parents can have an illegal abortion and the army is none the wiser. But those who cannot pay have no recourse but to turn to their Women's Corps officers for help. Much then depends on the officer. Some quietly help and refer the matter no higher up the line. Others help but report to their superiors. Still others go by the book—in which case the woman is released with the double stigma of early army discharge and illegitimate pregnancy.

For the majority of women soldiers, the army is less a matter of sexual adventure or misadventure than a life of gray routine, of twelve-hour stints at typewriter or switchboard. Although higher-status jobs such as intelligence collation, technician posts and radar vigilance are slowly opening up to women, with much pressure from C.O. Raz, most army women derive their job satisfaction in the army not from their work but from the company they keep. Parachute folding is therefore seen as more glamorous than intelligence work though it is deadly dull. The glory for women lies in the men around them, not in their own contribution to the I.D.F. Thus it is that the one-time recruiting slogan for the air force—*ha tovim la'tayis*, "the best boys to pilot training"— was given extra bite by army wits with the addition of *ha-tovot la'tayasim*, "the best girls to the pilots."

Those women who sign on for Israel's standing army after their regular two-year service generally enjoy more interesting and more responsible work, on the officers' level. Though marriage does not bar them from an army career, it does put them at a disadvantage in comparison with men. For instance, they receive smaller extra allowances on their salaries than men for marriage and family, the most striking difference being in housing. While married career army men automatically receive housing expenses, women have to fight to get them, and they receive less. Asked about this in the Knesset at the end of 1975, Defense Minister Shimon Peres made the situation crystal clear: "There is a distinction between the married man soldier and the married woman soldier. The reason for this is that the man is the head of the family and the main provider." Principle aside, Peres' statement is also untrue, since many young women sign up for a few years' army career in order to put their student husbands through college.

But the career army woman suffers more than diminished

economic benefits. Because she does not serve in combat, she commands neither the social status nor the respect accorded male officers in Israeli society. And this lack of status affects her post-army career. The smooth integration of the army in Israeli society as a whole enables top male career soldiers to play key roles in the industrial, bureaucratic and political establishment of the country after they retire at a relatively young age from the army. Political scientist Amos Perlmutter analyzed the occupations of retired senior I.D.F. officers and found that over half were in the top ranks of business, politics, government ministries and government corporations.[14] The army is a major resource for establishment personnel. But since women never rise above the level of colonel in the I.D.F., such post-army careers are virtually closed to them.

At lower levels too, I.D.F. women officers are disadvantaged in comparison with men. Male junior officers have the highest career mobility of any social group in Israel, within the army and after it, while for women an army career is rather a dead end. Male I.D.F. officers are encouraged to develop their potentialities for an alternative career, in such fields as economics and administration, while serving in the army. While such options are also open to the I.D.F.'s top women, they are available on neither so frequent nor so generous a scale. Thus while an army career is an excellent means to establish himself rapidly for a man, for a woman it is more a convenient means of earning a salary.

The crux of the problem is that women cannot serve in combat, the central concern of army life. The larger problem that overlies it is the tragic necessity for the centrality of the army in Israeli life. No one can tell how much longer this situation must continue, but while it does, very few Israeli women would even want to fight. Eager to emphasize their femininity, they prefer to see themselves as protected, not protectors. The few who do wish to take a full role in the I.D.F. do so for strong psychological reasons as well as for social, economic and political reasons. The guilt and anxiety experienced by many women during wartime is usually covered over by feminine rationalizations of a woman's role. But it found unusual expression in the person of Techiya Bat-Oren, who ran "advice" columns for women in the press and on the radio for years and then experienced a complete change of heart in middle age. "From hyper-anxiety for our daughters," she wrote, "we've turned them into dolls, and imposed a double burden of anxiety on the shoulders of our sons—for their own lives and those of their dolls. I do not want another war, but if it comes, I do not want any son or husband to be killed in my place. I want full equality of rights."[15]

If few women in the army want equal rights—and duties— there may be even fewer in that other bastion of the myth of liberation, the kibbutz. Equality is exactly what the modern kibbutz woman does not want. Although she lives in an environment designed in large part to "free the woman from the yoke of domestic service," as the old kibbutz slogan put it, the young kibbutz woman of today is determinedly setting about to change her environment so that she can again bear that yoke, this time of her own free will.

It seemed the ideal environment for women's liberation. Kibbutz women are economically independent of their husbands, both being full members of the kibbutz. With all cooking, laundering, sewing and so on done communally, and with children living apart from their parents in special children's houses, where they are cared for by trained nurses and teachers, the mother would be freed of domestic and maternal cares to devote her full energy to the commune. This tiny proportion of Israel's population (the kibbutz accounts for just over 3 percent of the total population, spread through nearly 240 kibbutzim throughout the country) appeared to have found the answer to what they still call "the biological tragedy of the woman." Or so, at least, it seemed. Today, far from having surpassed biology, kibbutz women are striving for a philosophy that will turn the "biological tragedy" into a blessing—the blessing of familism and of domesticity.

The problem begins at work. Kibbutz men work almost exclusively in the productive branches of the kibbutz economy —agriculture and industry. Because they earn revenue, these branches are high status. Socialist ideology notwithstanding, the service branches of the kibbutz—kitchen, laundry, school —are low status, since they produce no revenue. And this is where the women work. Sex typing in work has now reached the extreme of up to 90 percent of men working in production, and up to 90 percent of women in the services. For example, in the most radical of the three main kibbutz movements, the Artzi movement, 87 percent of those working in agriculture are men.[16] Women may work for short periods of time in poultry, vegetable gardening and hothouse culture, which are considered suitable areas for them. These are mainly young women, high schoolers who are performing what kibbutz sociologist Yonina Talmon described as a "mandatory rite of passage" in agricultural work before settling down into marriage and domestic work.[17] In the Ichud and Meuchad movements, always far less explicit than the Artzi in their ideology of sexual equality, the sex typing is still stronger. In kibbutz industries, women are only 23 percent of personnel, and then mainly in "female" industries such as ceramics, arts and crafts, and textiles. In the construction branch and auxiliary services, women make up a brave 1 percent of personnel.

On the other side of the fence, women are 84 percent of the Artzi complement of housekeeping and education personnel. Some men are employed in general maintenance and gardening, and men become more frequent in the educational system as the grade level rises, so that while there are practically no men in kindergarten teaching, men are 40 percent of kibbutz high-school teachers. In the Ichud and Meuchad movements, the percentages are higher. They represent the near culmination of a progression toward complete sexual polarization in work. In the Ichud movement, the most conservative, about half the women worked in production in the twenties, 15.2 percent in 1949, 10.4 percent in 1954, and some 9 percent today. Polarization is learned on the kibbutz: it is greater among kibbutz-born people than among those who joined a kibbutz as children or adults. And an interesting sidelight is that more women cross the sex barrier into "male" work than men into "female" work. Talmon sees men working in "female" tasks as a symbolic atonement for sex discrimination. But it is, as she notes, a token.

Far from being disappointed, the women show an eager desire for femininity over feminism, constantly stressing the "natural" and "instinctual" traits of women. Miriam, a young mother in Kibbutz Beit Alpha, remarks, "What's the importance of sex equality? I was born on a kibbutz and never felt any need for equality of the sexes. The division of work and roles is natural, and I have no feeling of discrimination."[18] Shlomit, an older woman writing in the Artzi weekly newspaper, puts it more pompously: "A social framework does not change fundamentally, and the woman in the kibbutz has certainly not changed. She remains the same splendid woman at the center of whose world is her family and children. The ambition to be compared to men, which we had when the movement was still young, was the immature silliness of a stormy and visionary time."[19]

Menahem Rosner, a sociologist who runs the Artzi research center in Kibbutz Givat Haviva, ran a cross-cultural study in which he found that kibbutz members were more extreme in their sex typing than other people. Only 15 percent of kibbutz members thought that being an electrician could be a suitable occupation for both sexes, for example, whereas in France, 38 percent thought it could be. Only 18 percent on kibbutz thought that a driver could be either sex; in France, 62 percent thought so.[20] Many kibbutzim, in fact, still do not allow women members even to apply for driving licenses, arguing that it is a waste of time and even harmful, since one of the main forms of driving on kibbutz—tractor driving—is staunchly believed to cause infertility. Two women driving into the seashore kibbutz Ein Carmel to visit a friend were welcomed by a young boy who asked how they had arrived. They pointed to their car. "But," he asked, "are you men or women?" "You can see we're women," they replied. "Why do you ask?"

"Well, if you're women, where's the man who drove you here?"

During the Yom Kippur War, the first time since 1948 that Israel experienced a long period of national emergency with men in reserve military service for several months, this policy spelled economic disaster for some kibbutzim, mainly young ones with no post-army-age men to drive the tractors. The high-school students who shouldered most of the "male" work did not know how to drive, and neither did the women. There was no one to haul in the crops from the fields or to get the milk containers to the dairy. Despite such problems, Rosner found only 6 percent of kibbutz members who thought that women should be allowed to drive tractors.

The crisis of the Yom Kippur War was a tragic but appropriate opportunity for women to reassert their capabilities. It was ignored. The emergency merely dramatized the situation. Rosner found that no women moved into production in the majority of Artzi kibbutzim, and in the rest very few women moved into male jobs.[21] The high-school students shouldered most of the burden. The picture was similar in the Ichud and Meuchad movements. Lionel Tiger and Joseph Shepher, an anthropologist-sociologist team, looked at six kibbutzim during the emergency months following the outbreak of the Yom Kippur War. They found that in two kibbutzim the number of women in male work rose slightly, in two it remained the same, and in the two others it actually fell, resulting in overstaffing of the kitchen and the children's home as the women flocked to protect the nest.[22] Sexual polarization is by now so deep on the kibbutz that not even the extreme crisis of war can induce women to work in production.

Kibbutz-born women have a mass of rationalizations. "Working outdoors ages your skin prematurely—just look at all the wrinkles on the older women who worked outdoors in the old days," says one young woman, whose strained face speaks of wrinkles soon to come. The supposed ravages of sun and fresh air on female skin reveal a high consciousness of cosmetic beauty in kibbutz women. There is hardly a kibbutz that does not have a beauty parlor—an abomination and unforgivable bourgeois luxury in the old days. But whether they work indoors or out, kibbutz women still find that the wrinkles appear. And their fight is against wrinkles, not against discrimination. They see no beauty in the warm, lively eyes of the older women for whom ideals were more important than crow's-feet, and prefer the sterile, skin-deep beauty of the cosmetician to the wrinkled radiance of those older women.

Sex typing in education, so rigorously avoided by early ideologues, has seeped back. In kibbutz kindergartens, girls play with dolls and boys with tractors, just like their city counterparts, and teenage girls take rhythm classes while the boys practice on the basketball court. Advah, a young kindergarten teacher in Merhavia, one of the oldest Artzi kibbutzim, reacted to the idealistic purity of a new Artzi kibbutz, Kerem Shalom in the Negev, where teachers are trying to avoid sex typing: "What do they want to do to the children? Raise a generation of lesbians and homosexuals?"[23] Ilana, education coordinator of the Artzi kibbutz Gal-On, less rigid than Advah, drew up a list of young men ready to work in the kindergarten and presented it to the kibbutz secretary: "I don't know if he ever actually read the list, but he certainly didn't take it seriously. He said that this was the way to turn the kibbutz into a circus."[24] In a Galilee kibbutz, a young male volunteer from the States wanted to work in the children's house. The rumor spread that he was a homosexual; that was the only explanation for such "unmanly" aspirations. He was rejected and soon afterward left the kibbutz.

Individual exceptions can be found. Some have become legends within the kibbutz movements, their fame proving their exception to the rule. One exception is a woman in her fifties who works in the cowshed of her kibbutz, and whose six-year-old grandson was amazed to find her there when he wandered in one day. "What are you doing here?" he asked. "But you know I work in the cowshed," replied his grandmother. "Oh yes, but I thought you just made coffee and sandwiches for the men, not that you actually did the work yourself."

By ages seventeen and eighteen, the mouths are no longer

those of babes. Kibbutz psychologist A. I. Rabin found that more than half the items on the Maudsley neuroticism scale (a large inventory of items measuring anxiety and social adaptation) differentiated between teenage boys and girls, with the girls consistently more moody, tense and anxious, more sensitive, more given to daydreaming, more tired and lonely. While the boys thought there were plenty of interesting jobs for everyone on the kibbutz, the girls said that there were not enough for women. And where the boys agreed that "the girl enjoys taking care of a household more than most other jobs in the kibbutz," the girls were far less enthusiastic about their future service role. Rabin concluded that "the girls are less well adjusted to the kibbutz than the boys."[25]

But maybe it is the kibbutz that is less well adjusted to them. Differences in school achievement between boys and girls are far greater on the kibbutz than in the city. The disparity appears at about age eleven and increases until by eighteen kibbutz boys are better than girls in nearly all subjects.[26] In their teens, kibbutz women are already retreating rather than fighting. Aware of the domestic and service roles awaiting them, they start restricting their interests from an early age, resigning themselves to acceptance of their "female" role in kibbutz life.

While they persuade themselves that the services are where they want to be, kibbutz women are there more by pressure of circumstance than by choice. As the kibbutz grew larger, as more children were born, as the demand for more sophisticated services grew—in other words, as the kibbutz became more established—nobody questioned that those women in production would leave it to take over the domestic side of affairs. The dissonance between egalitarian ideology and discriminatory reality is bridged by the argument of "nature," an argument used to demonstrate that while the ideology is theoretically correct, it is unattainable in practice, since women are best suited to the traditional roles.

Kibbutz women have those roles with a vengeance. While the city housewife has a wide range of tasks to do at her own pace, the kibbutz woman is shouldered into one specific aspect of housework. Either she cooks full-time, or sews full-time, or launders full-time, or looks after young children full-time. Even the variety of housework is taken away from her. Rather than broadening her work horizons, the kibbutz has limited them still further than the traditional housewife role. The once anticipated "emancipation of women from the yoke of domestic service" has boomeranged with the dull thud of boredom.

"Instinct," "nature" and "the character of woman" are the phrases in popular use. It is on the kibbutz that the biological and "real woman" myths are strongest. "You can't have men looking after children," says one young mother, "they just wouldn't know what to do, when women know it naturally." "It is natural that the mother tend more toward the family and the man toward work," says another. "It is a part of nature and it's impossible to determine whether it's desirable or not," says a third. And in a still more extreme vein than this blunt refusal to look at the issue, another mother states that "the difference is natural and it would be a bad thing if social activities took precedence over the family for the woman."

The vast majority of kibbutz women agree. And they have acted accordingly. The children's house, once one of the central institutions of kibbutz life, is fast disappearing as kibbutz after kibbutz takes the decision to have children sleep in their parents' home. Nearly all Ichud kibbutzim and many Meuchad kibbutzim now have family housing, thus creating for the mother the same double burden of outside work plus housework as in many urban families. And yet the demand for family housing has come from the women, with the men tagging on behind. Many men resisted it at first, for not only does it, at one stroke, undermine the communality of kibbutz life, but it is also an expensive step to take, requiring construction of new housing roomy enough for families instead of couples, and a cutback in women's work hours so that they can tend to their home and children. The preference of family over community is now so strong in many kibbutzim that the only time the whole kibbutz eats together in the communal dining hall is on the festive Friday night—the Sabbath meal. The rest of the time many families cook in their own homes, or take food from the communal dining hall to be eaten at home.

Economically, ideologically and socially the move to family housing contradicts the very raison d'être of the kibbutz. It may also be one of the first major signs (another is the use of hired labor in kibbutz industries) of the end of the kibbutz as an institution. For the direction is toward a farm or industry cooperatively owned by families from private homes.

Even the more radical Artzi movement has started family housing in some of its kibbutzim. As a whole the movement is fighting a rearguard action, and many Artzi members feel it is only a matter of time until family housing is fully accepted in their movement too. At present Artzi women, like women in the other two movements, tend to refuse work or chances to study outside the kibbutz, since that would mean that they could not be with their children during the day. Even in those kibbutzim without family housing, the women stress this argument, since if they worked outside the kibbutz they would not be available for the *shaat ha-ahava*—the "hour of love" in the middle of each morning which mothers of young children take off to spend with their children. Esther, one of the founders of the Artzi kibbutz Yehiam in the foothills of the Galilee, which was started in 1946, reflects: "We thought the new generation would be more open and liberated, but they're turning out quite the opposite..." She draws hard on her cigarette, sighs, and concludes, "They're deliberately retreating into the nuclear family."

Having sown the seeds of an egalitarian utopia, founding mothers such as Esther have seen a domestic one bloom for their daughters. They sit and try to analyze where they went wrong at Yehiam. Some blame themselves for not trying harder, as Esther does. Others, like Rachel, say that "perhaps we never really wanted equality for our daughters. We talk with pride of how we once worked in agriculture, but we really don't want our daughters to. We want things to be better, to be easier for them. . . ." And yet others, like Ruthy, attribute the swing to the generation gap, to a reaction of daughters against mothers. None, however, questions the devotion of the kibbutz as a whole to the ideology of sexual equality. They watch, resigned and somewhat disillusioned, as marriage and birth rates, both higher in kibbutzim than the Israeli average, rise, and as the divorce rate, lower on kibbutz than in the rest of Israel, falls. Their daughters, the young women of today's kibbutzim, are firmly entrenching themselves in the family and home, enthusiastically taking on the double burden that their mothers and grandmothers tried to discard.

It is the founding mothers who are the few politically active women on the kibbutz. Women attend the weekly general assemblies far less often than men, and women in the twenty to thirty-five age group rarely go. When there, they rarely speak: "We sit and knit or embroider and afterwards we gossip," says one old-timer, with a resigned smile. Women are rarely elected to the three central kibbutz positions— kibbutz manager, treasurer and kibbutz secretary. Over 90 percent of these posts are held by men, and when women are elected it is generally only when a fourth position is added to the central committee. If a woman is elected kibbutz secretary, a fourth position is often created in order to have a male secretary as well. In the small committees that run the various branches of kibbutz life women are overrepresented on the culture and education committees, which inevitably have male chairmen on the argument that only a man can get along well with the all-male executive. On all other committees, they are badly underrepresented. Finance committees are generally all male.

Two reasons are most often heard for women's noninvolvement in kibbutz politics: that they do not want to be elected and that they have no time. Both are true. Women do not want to be elected because they feel unable to handle a position of general responsibility in the kibbutz—a position requiring especially detailed knowledge of the productive branches, with which they have practically no experience.

They still feel that service work is where women should be; the main problem for them is not sex typing, but the low status of nonproductive "female" work. And so they have fallen back on the one assured method of asserting their productive status: production in the form of reproduction.

Bearing and rearing children is the one female role on the kibbutz whose value is unquestioned. And as their opportunities for work satisfaction decrease with their confinement in a narrow subsector of service work, kibbutz women have demanded greater satisfaction from their role as mothers. It is as mothers that they seek the self-respect that is missing in the rest of their lives.

There is no lack of academic encouragement of this retreat into the family. The most notorious rationalization is put forward by anthropologists Tiger and Shepher in their book *Women in the Kibbutz*,[27] where they argue that kibbutz women are not in retreat but are searching out their natural role in life as women and mothers. This sociobiological determinism fits well with kibbutz women's own ideas on biology and women's role in society, giving them "scientific" backing in developing their femininity at the expense of ideology and of the concept of the kibbutz as a whole.

The death knell of the myth of sexual equality in the kibbutz, and yet the first sign of a possible awakening, came with the formation in 1975 of what once would have seemed the ultimate anomaly—a feminist consciousness-raising group in a small and struggling Artzi kibbutz. The group was founded by newcomers from North America, who were shocked at what they found on their arrival at Kibbutz Harel in the Judean foothills. "Kibbutz women aren't interested in equality; they're just interested in children," Ilana Dorfman, the group's founder, said in exasperation. "We came here thinking that the socialist ideology included sexual equality, but it obviously doesn't." Her words are reminiscent of those of the pioneer Sarah Malchin in 1913: "There [in Palestine] there was to be no distinction between men and women," but "our beautiful dreams were destroyed."[28] Today, Ilana continues, "it's not enough our trying to move, as a group, into agricultural production. There has to be a reciprocal movement on the part of the men. The sociological question of who is responsible for the family must be dealt with, and a clear ideological re-definition made."

The problem is that the sociological question has already been answered by kibbutz women, de facto, and the redefini-tion in effect made. In both cases it is in the direction that the Harel group and the early pioneer women would most abhor. In the place where feminists had thought their ideal could flower, the feminine mystique is now ripening as fast as the corn in the fields.

7

Marriage:
The National Panacea

"The whole of Israel is one big yiddishe
mama."
                              —Shuli,
                              thirty-three and single

The wedding is due to start at eight P.M. The first guest arrives somewhat naively just before eight, and wanders around listlessly watching a few other punctual stragglers arrive. By eight thirty the large wedding hall, rented for the occasion, is half full, and the guests are hungrily eyeing the long tables laden with cold cuts, fruit, dips, crackers, nuts, cakes and other delicacies according to the origin and pocket of the parents concerned. Some minutes later the bride arrives, in full white dress and almost unrecognizable under the special wedding makeup and coiffure which five assistants in the wedding salon took five hours to create that afternoon. She is somewhat tired from rushing around the city being photographed with her husband-to-be at various cultural sites, but tries not to show it.

In Jerusalem the couple and their photographer will have made the rounds of the Montefiore windmill in Yemin Moshe, the Knesset, the Israel Museum and the Western Wall; in Tel Aviv, the Helena Rubenstein pavilion, Old Jaffa and the sunset shimmering sea. The fathers of the couple hover eagerly around the milling guests, two to four hundred by now, welcoming each one and tactfully directing them to the special anteroom where they deposit the presents, hopefully checks, which they have brought with them. The mothers station themselves on each side of the high white chair on which the bride sits until the ceremony starts, welcoming guests. When the children in the crowd can no longer resist temptation and have started picking off the delicacies at the edge of the tables —by which time the early arrivals already have a glazed look of hunger and thirst—the groom enters. The bride moves to the wedding canopy, the groom joins her with both sets of parents, and the ceremony begins. It is short and concise. The groom takes the bride to be his sanctified property, the rabbi pronounces his blessing, the *ketuba* (the traditional marriage contract) is read, drinks are broken out, and the rush to the tables begins. As the guests wine and dine, the musicians start up full blast—Greek music at Oriental weddings, Israeli and Yiddish folk songs at Ashkenazi weddings. And whether Sephardi or Ashkenazi, rich or poor, they inevitably end the evening with a rousing hora—one of the few times that Israelis still dance their national dance.

This is the Israeli way of marriage, and it has made big business out of weddings in modern Israel. Renting a wedding hall, getting photographs taken, ordering flowers, beautifying the bride, renting her gown, hiring caterers, paying the musicians, printing invitations and a host of other expenses drive the cost of an average Israeli wedding up to over $4,000—a year and a half's average salary. Building contractors suddenly rich from the post-1967 building boom have spent up to $10,000 on a wedding.[1] And though a small minority of Israelis still prefer the speed of a small ceremony at the Rabbinate offices, or the warmth and intimacy of a wedding held at home, most insist on the show and status of a large-scale extravaganza, which may involve the parents in debt for several years.

Parents consider the show eminently worth the outlay. It is the sign that they have done right by their children, that they have seen them through childhood and into marriage in the accepted and established manner, and that they themselves are sufficiently well established to afford that manner. There also seems to be an almost magical belief that the greater the financial outlay, the greater the assurance of permanence of the match.

Israel is a married society par excellence. By age forty, only 2.5 percent of women have not married (4.9 percent in the U.S.) and 4.7 percent of men (8.3 percent in the U.S.). Marriage is Israel's national panacea. It provides security and stability in a country of recurring crises, which reinforce dependence on a stable nuclear unit. It provides a sense of continuity within the Jewish tradition, where a man who does not marry is considered as having shed innocent blood (since he bucks the Biblical commandment to "be fruitful and multiply"). And it provides a new sense of permanence for a people still traumatized by the experience of the Holocaust.

The Orthodox Jewish religion, the bourgeois norms of Eastern European immigrants after World War Two, and the Orientalism of those who came from Islamic countries have a common factor: their high stress on marriage and family as early priorities in the life process. Concern with marriage cuts across the boundaries of cultures and traditions to create a near consensus on the personal, social and national importance of the family.

Above all, marriage is the key to the strong symbolism of home in a homeland reborn, home for a people haunted by memories of their homes destroyed. It holds the promise of establishing material roots—an apartment, children, property —and offers the reassurance of permanence. For not only do Israelis nearly always get married; they generally stay married.

Despite claims in the American press of a "forty percent divorce rate" in Israel,[2] or of Israel's having the world's highest divorce rate next to Rhodesia,[3] divorces in Israel have been at a remarkably stable low since the early sixties. While 6.9 percent of women and 4.7 percent of men are divorced at age forty in the U.S., comparable figures for Israel are only 3 percent and 1.5 percent. In 1974 the U.S. divorce rate was

4.6 per thousand population, in Great Britain it was 2.1, in Sweden it was 3.1—and in Israel 0.9.[4] This places Israel midway on the scale of international divorces, far below the U.S. and most of Europe. Moreover, as the annual number of marriages has risen in Israel, alongside the increase in population, the annual number of divorces has remained peculiarly consistent, at around 2,500.

Israel's reputation as a high-divorce country is a perfect example of how a striking fact gets caught in peoples' minds even though it may no longer be true. In the years prior to the establishment of the State, and in the two or three years after 1948, Israel did indeed have the highest divorce rate in the world. In 1937, divorces ran at an astonishingly high 7.16 per thousand Jewish population. But this reflected the national rather than the emotional politics of the time, for it was the result of fictitious marriages contracted in Cyprus and elsewhere abroad to circumvent the British Mandatory quota on Jews entering Palestine. Women could enter Palestine as wives of men who held entry visas, and therefore married with the understanding that they would divorce on reaching their destination. By 1950 the rate had dropped to 2.1—still extremely high for the world at that time. But once again, it indicated more about the political and social conditions of Israel's birth than any deep-seated dis-ease among the new Israelis. Many of these divorces were also the results of Cyprus marriages, but Cyprus marriages of a different kind.

After World War Two, when the British Mandate closed Palestine to refugees from the Nazi regime and sent them back to their deaths, the Mandate imposed an almost total clampdown on Jewish immigration. Those caught attempting illegal immigration were detained in camps in Cyprus, where they waited until the gates were finally opened in 1948, and where they contracted well-intentioned marriages which contained, at their inception, the seeds of divorce. Some married idealistically, eager to start a new life and leave the old behind, sometimes marrying people with whom they had hardly a language in common, often only a few words of freshly learned Hebrew. Others married out of guilt, eager to make good to Holocaust survivors. And others simply felt that after the vast destruction of the Holocaust there was no time to waste, that they must marry and start new families as quickly as possible, even if they had not yet reached the promised land. Whether contracted out of idealism, guilt, or a driving need to see the Jewish people reborn in the most literal sense, such marriages, born under the intense pressure and boredom of detainee camp life, often could not withstand the reality of immigration and settlement in the new State of Israel, which was far from being the envisaged land of milk and honey. By 1960 the divorce rate had settled down to 1.1 per thousand population, and has been slowly decreasing ever since.*

The universality and stability of marriage in Israel is due in large part to women's acceptance of the exclusive housewife and mother role, and to the pragmatism with which Israelis choose their marriage partners. Psychologist Esther Goshen-Gottstein, working in the mid-sixties, found that 46 percent of Israeli women married because they wanted their own home, 38 percent because it was expected of them, 28 percent because they wanted children, 13 percent so as not to be alone, and 11.5 percent for love and sex (many gave more than one answer).[5] Women living a modern life-style, mainly Ashkenazi, most emphasized the desire for their own home, and stressed love and sex more often than did the traditional women from Oriental backgrounds, for whom social expectations were the main reason for marriage. Sociologist Rivka Bar-Yosef forced largely middle-class Tel Aviv women to choose among reasons for their marriage in a 1974 survey, and found that only 45 percent reported having married for love, 25 percent because it was "the thing to do," 15 percent to get a house and children, and 10 percent because of parental pressure.[6]

---

* The Cyprus marriage is still alive and well in a third manifestation: couples forbidden to marry under the civilly binding halachic rulings of the Rabbinate, lacking any possibility of civil marriage in Israel, take a trip to the nearest foreign country, Cyprus—if they can afford it—and marry there. The difference with latter-day Cyprus marriages is that they rarely end in divorce.

Pragmatism is the order of the day. "Parents don't live forever, so a woman has to have a home of her own," said a Persian woman from a traditional background. "One has to build one's home and leave one's past family," as a modernistic Israeli-born woman put it. This down-to-earth shunting aside of the romantic—and considerably less stable—aspect of marriage is also reflected in the qualities women look for in a husband. For traditional women the qualities are framed in the negative—not a criminal, not a card player, not a girl chaser, not a wife beater—while modern women stress love and understanding far more, with a particularly high emphasis on compatibility. They look, says Goshen-Gottstein, for a congenial type of personality who could be described as quiet, decent, cultured, warm-hearted, intelligent and considerate, exactly the kind of man that novelist Amos Oz depicted so poignantly in the character of the husband in *My Michael*.[7]

Michael, as depicted by Oz, is the man Robert Graves advocates for the "real woman," the "simple affectionate husband" who cannot understand her. This is precisely Hannah's dilemma in *My Michael*, but rather than reassure her in her womanhood, it contributes to her slow progression across the border from acceptably schizoid to full withdrawal and a life of complete fantasy. Shockingly described once as tracing "a typical Israeli marriage of the nineteen-fifties,"[8] *My Michael* provided an identification figure for modern Israeli women when it was published in 1968. It became an immediate bestseller in Israel, a book which no woman with any pretensions to intellectualism would dream of reading less than twice. And yet it describes the failure of the security of marriage, the failure of her husband's decency, quietness and consideration to satisfy Hannah's craving for passion.

"I am writing this because people I loved have died. I am writing this because when I was young I was full of the power of loving, and now that power of loving is dying. I do not want to die," she says in the novel's opening paragraph. Her despair and sense of estrangement within the security of marriage recur: "Will we die, Michael, you and I, without touching each other so much as once?" she asks near the end. "You are a stranger, Michael. You lie next to me at night, and you are a stranger." Hannah finds her passion by rejecting the reality of her Michael for a rich and dangerous fantasy life, until the fantasies are more real than the world about her. By the end, the sexuality of her visions of the Arab twins she knew as a girl, now transformed in her mind into terrorists, is clear. It derives its power not only from the sense of escape from the humdrum normality of existence, but also from the excitement of betrayal, of betraying her husband with the enemy.

The same syndrome of escape into fantasy and withdrawal, the last struggles against resignation and despair, recurs throughout the work of Israel's women novelists and story writers. In Amalia Kahana-Karmon's *And Moon in the Valley of Ayalon* the atmosphere is one of constriction and erosion, with the heroine reaching out for love in an extramarital affair only to be disappointed again. In Shulamit Har-Even's stories of married women in love, they flee from reality into self-love, or into a wild illusory world where they can fantasize their actions by will.

Yet though the security of marriage may be potentially maddening, it is the rare Israeli woman who dares to buck the marriage system for a life of her own. "You don't have to marry!" exclaims actress Miriam Eron in *Nashim Odot Nashim (Women About Women)*, a play staged by five women who had gotten together to work on theater games and found a performance that evolved out of their problems as women. Miriam, thirty-two and single, comes up with this revelation in the play as if she had, in the Hebrew slang term, discovered America. She is tired, she explained after one performance, of the whole game of asking, in each relationship, "What's in it for me? Will it lead to marriage?" "There's an early drive to build the nest and to accept the one accepted life-style—that of young couples living separated, isolated lives," she says.

But her discovery evokes no response from her audiences. You do have to marry in Israel, and the earlier the better in order to save all parties involved—parents, relatives, friends and acquaintances—unnecessary worry and anxiety. "We're

only one generation removed from our East European and North African parents," says Eron, "and the materialistic value system is still exactly the same. The drive is to establishment, as quickly as possible."

The pressure to marry starts early, and the average marriage age is now twenty-one for women and twenty-four for men. The average age for marriage among Oriental Jews has risen slightly, and that for Western-origin Jews has gradually lowered, so that the two are presently converging in a national consensus on the right age to marry. By age seventeen, marriage is at the top of Israeli girls' list of priorities. In a large-scale research survey published in 1976,[9] Rivka Bar-Yosef found that seventeen-year-old girls have already formed a clear picture of their expectations in life, and that the more traditionally feminine the role, the more it is valued. The girls were asked to rate the importance of success in seven fields, and the results were so striking that it is worth giving them in full:

	NOT IMPORTANT	IMPORTANT	VERY IMPORTANT
motherhood	7.6%	23.6%	68.8%
housewife	5.7%	25.9%	68.4%
feminine appearance	16.8%	40.5%	42.7%
helping professional advancement of husband	22.2%	36.7%	41.1%
professional activity	31.3%	42.1%	26.6%
voluntary activity	59.0%	27.1%	13.9%
public activity	86.4%	10.4%	3.2%

The outside columns show a clear ranking of the myths in Israeli women's lives: "biological" roles first, "real woman" roles next, "liberated" roles last.

These seventeen-year-olds would be oddly insensitive to the society in which they live if they were not acutely aware

of the importance of marriage for them. The pressure toward
the marital norm is so strong that Shuli, an attractive thirty-
three-year-old who is unmarried, describes the whole country
as "one big yiddishe mama." If a woman is still unmarried by
age twenty-five (a man may get grudging leeway until his late
twenties), this pressure peaks to panic, a panic that then grips
the woman herself. In anticipation, the search for a marital
partner is generally assumed to be well under way by the
time a girl leaves high school, or at the latest, by the time she
leaves the army, if she goes into it. It is an anxiety-fraught
process, made all the sharper by rumors of a shortage of
available young men.

While statistics show that there are more single men than
women up to age thirty, mothers and single daughters persist
in believing that there are fewer. Women tend to marry men
two or three years older than they, so that a certain temporary
statistical imbalance did arise due to the post-1948 baby boom,
which resulted in a greater number of women approaching
marriageable age in the late sixties than there were men two
or three years older than they. By now, however, the situation
has evened out. The cold light of statistics reflects none of the
drastic threats voiced by young women who regale the listener
with the numbers of those fallen in Israel's wars. The numbers are high but do not indicate a serious imbalance in the
sexual ratio.

Mothers and daughters entering the marriage sweepstakes
are encouraged in their panic by the *shadchanim*—professional
matchmakers whose computerized lists are an extension of the
traditional role of the *shadchan* of the East European shtetl.
They play on the marriage panic with statistics that show a
shortage of "suitable" available men. Tel Aviv has twelve
established matchmaking firms and Jerusalem three, all doing
nicely out of the market panic they help create. Modern Israelis of all classes and pockets go to the *shadchanim:* their
"success rate" is high. In the old days the *shadchan* succeeded
since it was accepted in shtetl society that this was the way one
married—for reasons of common sense, family bonding, social
background and status rather than romance. The modern

shadchan succeeds because he appeals to the same pragmatism in young Israelis. Miriam, a twenty-two-year-old science student who has no regular boyfriend, says, "It's an excellent system, the *shadchan*. Marriage is far too important a thing to leave to chance. You want to ensure that you get married to the right type of person, so you define what you want, approach it scientifically, and let the expert handle it. It makes perfect sense."

Where the shtetl *shadchan* received his fee in the form of a percentage of the marriage dowry established by custom, today's *shadchan* charges by the year (about $50) and claims a bonus ranging from $250 to $400 if he succeeds. If marriage hopefuls cannot afford the professionals, they can do it themselves in the small-ads sections of the Hebrew press. There columns headed *Shiduchim* (matches) sometimes list hundreds of items in the end-of-the-week Friday papers. "Interested in a rich American or European girl up to age twenty-five," says one ad, reflecting the businesslike Israeli eager to find a new immigrant with *zchuyot*—immigrant privileges giving rights to buy household goods tax-free and to get large mortgages on apartments.

Most ads give the age and height (in centimeters) of the advertiser. "Bachelor, 25/168, nice and established, looking for a suitable girl," or "26/174, plus car, plus apartment, looking for serious traditional girl." The ads placed by women are somewhat more teasing: "Girl soldier, 18, sweet and humane," or "28/129, European and serious, interested in meeting you." Sometimes the demands are so precise that one wonders at the advertiser's designs. Why should a woman "24/165" be searching for a man of "33/170"? If such detail is too scanty, and if a marriage prospect has a taste for publicity, she or he can also write in to the army radio station and perhaps be accepted for their once-monthly matchmaking program *A Man and a Woman*. The candidate states her or his preferences and then answers phone calls on the air from prospective mates, sometimes making dates on the spot.

But at no charge and with no national publicity, though with much noise and gossip, relatives, friends and mere acquaintances are always on the lookout for a suitable *shiduch* for their daughters, sons, or friends. Many take pride in their success in this field, and will tick off on their fingers the number of couples they have brought together—with a finger flicked back into place here and there for a *shiduch* that ended in divorce.

Few such marriages do end in divorce, however, not only because of the fear of being alone, which Israelis equate with loneliness, but also because young couples tend to have their first child within the first year or two of marriage, and the second soon after. Once there are children, divorce is largely out of the question. Sociologist Bar-Yosef found that 65 percent of Tel Aviv women thought that a couple should divorce if they quarrel all the time—as long as there are no children. If there are children, however, 60 percent say no divorce, however bad the arguments are. Answering a question on why children are important, 61 percent said that they give meaning to life—perhaps the same 60 percent of women who thought children barred divorce.[10]

Divorce threatens the stability that Israelis try to establish in their personal lives. The no-risk policy which most young Israelis follow on their road to establishment cannot accommodate divorce. And their society does not easily accommodate it either. Their social lives have been extraordinarily stable since childhood, with close-knit peer groups from kindergarten and school through the army and on into adult life. Israeli relationships, sexual or nonsexual, tend to last many years, and rarely end in sudden breaks. If they do occur, such breaks are hard to take, not only for the divorced couple but also for their friends. Ezer Weizmann, when he was head of the Israeli air force, told journalist Zeev Schiff, "If a pilot of mine divorces unnecessarily, I must intervene, because otherwise it hits at his morale and at the general morale of the air force."[11]

The experience of army service also has a sobering effect on young Israelis. The closeness to matters of life and death and the high risk sometimes incurred in army service are compensated for—often overcompensated—in the search for low-risk security in personal lives. It is almost as if Israelis skip those few precious years of rebellion after high school and into the early twenties, years which American and European youth often spend in search of their own bents, selfishly indulgent perhaps, as Israelis see them, but also romantically explorative, searching for excitement and interest in life. Young Israelis want to settle down to as solid an everyday life as possible. And this means family life.

The recurring security crises reinforce the family. Each time friends are killed or wounded, couples fall back on each other for comfort and stability in the face of mortality and insecurity. Whereas such conditions elsewhere might create an atmosphere of "What does it matter anyway?" and a hedonistic living for the moment, in Israel they reinforce the attachment to any opportunity for permanence. Couples hang on, determined to make the best of it.

This is much easier to do when one's expectations from marriage are within reason. Rivka Bar-Yosef found that Israeli women look for mutual support and understanding in marriage rather than love or sex. On this basis over half report themselves "quite happy" in marriage, 38 percent very happy, and only 10 percent unhappy. Seventy-two percent reported that their expectations of marriage had been met, and only 9 percent that they definitely had not.[12] Their marriages are generally sensible arrangements of companionship rather than passion, of comfort and convenience, and of exigency rather than excitement.

Only a third of married women in Israel work outside the home, and the majority do so only because they need the income. Well over half of the Tel Aviv women surveyed by Bar-Yosef thought that the wife's working harms her husband, depriving him of a well-kept home. Eighty percent thought it harms the children, a figure which indicates a considerable amount of guilt among working mothers over the effect of their work on their families. In answer to what a woman should do if her husband feels neglected because she works, two thirds replied that she should work only part-time, 13 percent that she should stop, and 12 percent that the husband should change his attitudes. One percent advocated divorce.

The marriage pattern that Bar-Yosef found is extremely traditional: the wives are almost exclusively concerned with child care, the majority of husbands entering the scene only to discipline and for family outings. The family budget is exclusively the man's concern, and nearly all the women are quite content to leave those matters to their husbands.

This consensus, cutting across cultural and social lines, emerges from a truly formidable ethnic mix. Anthropologist Phyllis Palgi, who has followed the development of Israeli subcultures, emphasizes an emerging homogeneity where cultural pluralism and diversity might have been expected. She traces three main family types in the parent generation, those now in their late forties and fifties. All three are strongly familistic, though they have different internal patterns.[13]

The first type is the veteran Ashkenazi family, already in Israel by the time the State was declared in 1948, whose main aims are social and material establishment. These people often played an active role in establishing the State, and they still form the establishment of the country today. The second type is the isolated family of post-war European survivors. More than half of these came out of the ghettos or concentration camps, and many had spent the war years in flight or in hiding. The survivors—sometimes the sole survivors—of truncated families, their intense desire to rebuild their families after the trauma of World War Two was profoundly linked with a desire to regain some measure of material comfort after years of deprivation. The third type is the traditional Oriental (Sephardi) family from Islamic countries. Highly patriarchal, it combines the male exclusivity of the Jewish tradition with that of the Islamic tradition. The highest status belongs to the father, and next is the eldest son. The sole means by which the women, confined to the home, can gain a sphere of indirect power is through motherhood.

The specific patterns are now starting to converge. In veteran Ashkenazi families sons and daughters are intensifying family ties while those from Sephardi families are loosening theirs somewhat, to approach an Israeli norm. Today

Ashkenazi brides often prefer to set up house as near to their mothers as possible, a pattern far more typical of Sephardi families in the past. Israel's socioeconomic conditions considerably influence such change. Buying an apartment, for instance, is an important aspect of marriage in Israel. With little rental housing available, and what there is extremely expensive, young couples feel compelled to join in the race for property as soon as possible. What many young Sephardi couples, whose parents are generally unable to buy them an apartment, register for "young couples" apartments in new tower complexes being built on the outskirts of the cities and towns, young Ashkenazi couples often have parents sufficiently affluent to buy an apartment for them near the parents' homes. Thus looser kinship ties develop among previously very close Sephardi families, and ties are strengthened among veteran Ashkenazi families, who used to place more stress on the larger collective than on the nuclear family.

Another pattern once thought peculiar to Sephardi families is also spreading: the wife who stays home to be a full-time housewife and mother. Sephardi wives, out of necessity, now work far more than they used to, whereas the opposite trend is apparent among well-established young Ashkenazi couples. The ideal is that after the children are grown the Ashkenazi wife will find part-time work, but it rarely happens. By then the woman prefers to concentrate on grandmothering or to have another child, at age forty-plus, to fill the gap left by grown children or a dead son. These wives are generally well-educated, but their intellectual development, though it serves as a kind of insurance against the misfortune of a husband's death or divorce, serves less their own benefit than their husbands'. An intelligent wife, the reasoning goes, will understand her husband's problems better and give him the support he needs as he progresses at work. This characteristic of Israel's upper and upper-middle class—government officials, the free professions and upper-echelon army personnel—is becoming more frequent among other groups. Sephardi families have started to take greater pride in their daughters' education and even in their going into the army, where this is possible, chiefly because such achievements will enable them to find higher-status husbands.

Perhaps the clearest sign of the power of the family in Israel is the lack of any widespread, or at least overt, generational conflict. Young adult Israelis are not in rebellion *against* family but are moving *toward* a new Israeli family norm that incorporates some of their parents' patterns and some from other family types. The ease with which this integration is being achieved is indicated in the rapidly increasing rate of intercultural marriage, marriage between Ashkenazis and Sephardis. Practically unheard of when the State was founded, the rate of intercultural marriage now approaches a quarter of all marriages performed in Israel.

An increasingly common Israeli marriage pattern has been described by Jerry Berlin, a family therapist who now works as a psychologist in the Israeli army. In its "pure state," it crystallizes into an Israeli adaptation of Portnoyism, in which the wife-husband relationship develops into a mother-son one.

The transformation takes the marriage partners unaware. The wife finds herself "managing" her husband, and in so doing convinces herself that she is the power behind the throne. She cares for him, comforts him when he needs it, manipulates him when it serves her needs, and condones his sexual adventurism outside the marriage as a loving mother would her son's small peccadillos—though she keeps a weather eye open to ensure that these adventures lead to no serious involvement. Meanwhile she develops a smothering relationship with her real son, as if to ingest him and protect him from threat (a major threat being death in army service). Inevitably, all her hopes and ambitions devolve from her husband onto her son. While the former sees to her material comfort now, she depends on the latter for the pride that will add glow to her life. The glow of sexual satisfaction is sacrificed, and eventually her libido is invested entirely in her son.

There is a still darker side to Israeli marriage, once limited largely to Oriental families but now spreading to middle- and upper-class Ashkenazi families too: wife beating. Wife beating is often an accepted part of the Oriental marriage pattern, though one which young Oriental couples on the social ascent regard with disgust. It is such a widely accepted phenomenon in Israeli society that when Member of Knesset Marcia Freedman attempted to present a motion on the subject for the Knesset agenda in 1976 the almost exclusively male assembly found it hard to take her seriously. She was greeted with a wave of titters, guffaws and wisecracks, and a reply from Police Minister Shlomo Hillel that he saw no reason to place the problem of wife beating in Israel apart from the general problem of violence. Both Hillel and Justice Minister Haim Tzadok in fact voted against any Knesset action on the matter.

The precise extent of wife beating in Israel is unknown, but we do know that 85 percent of the women who turn to WIZO (a voluntary women's welfare organization) for help complain of having been beaten by their husbands. They have no recourse to any practical help, however. If they leave their husbands because of the beating, they can be accused under Jewish, and therefore civil, law of being a *moredet*, a rebellious wife, and divorced without child custody or any means of support. If they go to the police, they are inevitably told, "Lady, go home and make peace with your husband," since the police maintain a policy of not intervening in cases of family violence. Only if bones are broken will the police open a file, and even then action is rarely taken except in the most drastic cases. Any other form of public complaint on the part of the wife will bring on more beatings from her husband. Faced with this reign of terror and with a lack of elementary understanding, and in some cases with shame, beaten wives raise their hands in the all-too-familiar gesture of helplessness, and resign themselves. "If my husband says it's night when the sun is shining outside," says Zahava, a once-pretty thirty-year-old from Jerusalem's slum quarter of Musrara, who looks well over forty, "you'd better believe it's night, and anyone who says it isn't gets beaten."

Such women, mainly Oriental, are at the very bottom of Israel's social scale, the victims of their husband's own low social status. The only chance for these men to escape their own inferiority is at home, where they assert their authority with all the violence of those whose capability is continually questioned by the wider society in which they must function. It is the violence of those who feel powerless and must seek power in the most violent manner in the one place where they can find it—at home.

Oriental women therefore tend to concentrate on children as their life's satisfaction, expecting little from their husbands. "That's the way it is," as they say. They project the classic feminine image of traditional societies: dependent, passive and narcissistic in their unawareness of anything outside the small circle of their everyday lives. That they remain so is essential to their men. The men have the security of knowing that their home life is unchanging as they try to adapt to a modernizing society outside the home; the women's oppression is the means by which the men preserve some self-respect.

For such women, marriage is a fence that pens them into the world of the family. But for many others it is often a fence *against* the outside world, a secure retreat into care for others, husband and children, in return for material protection and the social status of marriage. The risks of boredom, withdrawal and even physical violence are accepted as part of the deal.

The security of marriage is also the women's mode of contributing to national security. A woman's husband, and later her sons, are her vicarious contribution to the national defense effort, a field of endeavor which takes priority over all others and from which she is automatically excluded as a wife and mother. Her menfolk become her "representatives" at the front, her link to Israel's defense.

The relationship of marriage to national security is sometimes expressed in the marriage ceremony itself. The rabbi may refer in his blessing to the need for a stable family life when Israel is under threat, or to the need for sons to carry on the tradition of Israel's army and ensure the country's security. In soldiers' weddings, the canopy is often held up by four rifles instead of the usual poles. It is the Israeli version of a common military custom, but its symbolism is far greater when the soldier may be called into action at any moment. Even the invitation can express the link: one that arrived recently in my mail was printed in the form of an I.D.F. reserve service call-up order.

Although marriage represents security for Israelis, it also entails unusual risks because of the national security situation. For women are widowed by war. This constant awareness gives an undercurrent of insecurity to the most outwardly secure marriages.

"Wherever we go there's always three: You, I and the next war," ran the satirical song written just after the Six Day War in 1967. The sentiment was shared by few at the time, but it is the prevalent feeling today. After the 1973 Yom Kippur War and the lack of any clear improvement in the security situation following it, there are few Israelis who do not foresee another war sooner or later. And just as few hold out any real hope of a war that would solve Israel's basic security problem. Over two and a half thousand Israeli men were killed in the Yom Kippur War. American experts forecast that Israeli casualties in another Middle East War would soar to over eight thousand dead.

The effects of war show first in a slight marriage boom after each one, and second in the number of widows in the country. While most war widows remarry as quickly as possible, not all manage to do so. Only 0.5 percent of men are widowed in both the U.S. and Israel; but 3.5 percent of the women are widowed in Israel, compared with 2.6 percent in the U.S. The extra 1 percent is made up largely of war widows.

Their dilemma is a difficult one, and an all-too-common one in this Jewish country. "Listen," says Sari, a widow from the Six Day War, whose mother was widowed in the Holocaust, "how can anyone ever be sure of anything in marriage? My grandmother was left a widow with six children, my mother was left a widow with three children, I was left a widow with one child. And now my daughter comes to me and says 'Mother, maybe I shouldn't ever marry so that I can escape this fate.' What am I meant to tell her? Maybe she's right. There's something almost mystical, predestined about it all, when·you really begin to think about it."

What makes things especially difficult in Israel is the extreme coupled-ness of Israeli society. The trauma of a husband's death is compounded by a descent in status. It is a descent that occurs slowly but inexorably. Immediately after a war, the war widows enjoy high status; they are the center of concern both in Israel as a whole and in their close circle of friends. But as the months wear on, their friends tend to drop away when faced with inviting an odd woman to a social gathering. The country returns to normal as the excitement or trauma of the last war recedes, and the widow is left to deal as best she can with her situation, usually by searching for another husband. She is painfully aware of the urgency of her search, not only because of her declining social status, but also because she knows that the next war is around the corner—how far away or how close no one can tell her—and that with that next war a new crop of war widows will absorb the remnants of a sympathy she still receives as a widow of the last war.

Most choose quickly, determined to find a new father figure for their children, and under heavy pressure from their family and friends to do so. But some, like Sari, rebel—for a while. "My mother found a good second husband right after the Second World War," she muses, "a man who would make a good father to me, since I was the only child that survived. But for herself she found nothing; there was no real love in her second marriage, she was just protecting herself. . . . I decided I wasn't going to do the same thing, and I made it alone for four years. And then I married again. Tami, my daughter, was a big factor—she was the only one at school without a father and she wanted, as children do, to be like everyone else. But it looks as if I went too fast. . . . Tell me, how can you live with someone under one roof for five years, five years we've been married now, without knowing how they feel? For what? I mean, why aren't we taught how to live alone?"

Sari went through a fairly common experience for attractive, newly widowed young women. "All the husbands of my friends started appearing at the door . . . alone." Exasperated by the pressure to remarry and by the assumption that a single woman must be sexually available, she packed and moved from Haifa to Tel Aviv. "Rumors still kept on coming back to me that had originated with my former friends, about who I was seeing, who I was just going to marry, and so on. But, you know, they didn't worry me too much. The minute they'd stop, then I'd have to look in the mirror and see what had happened," she says, curling her long dark hair through her fingers. "Right after the Six Day War everyone was terribly proud of me. Every social circle wanted its very own war widow in its midst. I'm glad I wasn't widowed after the Yom Kippur War. It was very different then. The pride in the war wasn't there, and I'm sure the widows felt it."

There is no trace of bitterness in her voice, just an acceptance of the situation as natural. Her second husband, like her first, is in the paratroop corps, the elite spearhead of the I.D.F. In another war, the chances of a paratroop officer would be cause for severe worry. Still, double widowhood by war, though known, is a rare phenomenon in Israel. The army generally tries to avoid sending a man married to a war widow to the front line, just as it avoids sending the only remaining son of parents of a dead soldier into battle.

"You know," she says, talking about a friend killed in a traffic accident, "every time something like that happens, you lose a part of yourself. A part of you dies. And then after a time you start wondering—how many parts of you are there? How long will it take for them all to die off, one by one, until there is nothing of you left? I don't know." Sari's words reflect something of the meaning of the word for widowhood in Hebrew, *almanut,* which originally also meant destitution. It comes from the same root as the word *almoni,* anonymous, reflecting the loss of identity experienced by a woman whose identity is completely linked with her husband's.

Sociologist Lea Shamgar-Hendelman, herself widowed in the 1948 War of Independence, has traced the patterns of what she calls "the trap of the war widows"—the loss of status with their sudden reversion to singlehood, and their reaction to it.[14] "The problem is that there's no place for a widow in Israeli society, it's so highly familistic," she says. Out of seventy-two widows she interviewed after the Six Day War, she found only one who said she would not remarry.

In the search for a new husband, status-consciousness is foremost. One widow who had been married to a career army lieutenant colonel put the problem in practical terms. "Look," she told Shamgar-Hendelman, "I want to get married again, but the problem is that I was married to a lieutenant colonel. Now lieutenant colonels and generals are often killed and so die before their wives, and that I don't want again, and in any case, how many single generals are there? Or how many single director generals of government ministries or any other comparable position?"

Among the war widows she talked to Hendelman found four main patterns, each with its own particular set of disadvantages. The first style is a full return to single status, in effect wiping the previous marriage off the slate. But this requires that the woman be young enough to be accepted in Israel's young world of premarriage, and that she have no children, or at least that she have parents who are willing to take the children to live with them while she leads her single life. In the second style, the woman takes on the special status of a war widow, which is highly effective for a short while after the war, but which tends to rise and fall in tune with Israel's security situation. It fades in the face of the next war, and thus is an extremely chancy long-term adaptation to widowhood. The third style, attempted by many widows of elite personnel, is to attempt to maintain previous status despite the husband's death. But the social connections which came as the fringe benefits of the husband's work become harder to sustain as time goes by, and within three years of the war, none of those who attempted this style had managed to maintain status. The fourth style is the search for status independent of the dead husband's, a style which requires considerable qualifications and which involves a serious catch, for the more successful the woman is professionally, the harder she will find it to remarry. Moreover, even though she could reach the same professional status as her dead husband, the social status that accrues to a man in that position does not come to her as a single woman. She faces a double loss of social status in payment for her professional status: the social benefits of professionalism are withheld from her while the possibility of remarriage becomes more remote as she is more successful.

The safest option for a war widow is chosen by the vast majority: remarriage as quickly as possible. Only this can offer her the social status and personal security which she lost in widowhood and bring her once again into the mainstream. Her problem is less the specific case of widowhood than the general one of singlehood in a highly coupled society: by the very universality of its acceptance, the panacea of marriage creates ills for those who, by force of circumstance or by their own free will, step outside its framework.

Being single in Israel today has the same aura of disaster as it did in Isaiah's prophecy of what would happen to Israel if it continued in its wicked ways: "And seven women shall take hold of one man in that day, saying, 'We will eat our own bread and wear our own clothes, only let us be called by your name; take away our reproach" (4:1). The war widows are well cared for by the Ministry of Defense; they have their own bread and their own clothing. But they still suffer the reproach of being unmarried. For them, the national panacea of marriage has created the very ills that it was intended to resolve.

Marriage is the reassurance that all is well with a man or a woman in Israel. "If he'd just get married and settle down, then he'd be a fine citizen," is what Israelis say about a single man in his late twenties. "She needs a husband and that will take care of all her problems," they say about a single woman. And to a cerain extent they are right, since marriage solves a host of social problems—problems that the concern with marriage creates. The single woman is often excluded from many forms of social gathering, for she is seen as a threat by married women, an enticement of their husbands. Though it rarely results in divorce if the threat does materialize, the single woman is an unnecessary risk. Cut off from the married mainstream of Israeli society, she turns her efforts toward getting married or remarried. For to be single, whether never married, divorced or widowed, is considered the greatest misfortune that can befall an Israeli woman. In the balance of professional against social life a single woman often sacrifices the former for the latter, even to the extent of withdrawing from a college doctoral program lest it affect her chance of marriage by placing her on too high a level. The exceptions, such as Golda Meir, who separated from her husband so that she could pursue her political career, merely prove the married rule. And the ills created by their exceptionality, by their rejection of the panacea, place their achievements in constant question, both for themselves and for other Israeli women. "Oh yes, I've paid a price to be what I am," Golda Meir once said, discussing the breakup of her marriage. "I've paid for it dearly."[15]

8

The Political Challenge

"Our aim is to turn feminists into politicians
and politicians into feminists."
—Lee Novick
vice-president of the
U.S. National Women's Political Caucus

On January 5, 1977, it was snowing in Jerusalem. Once mystical in its rarity in the Judean Hills, snow now falls nearly every year. As always, the snowed-in city had practically closed down. By evening the snowstorm had eased off, but forecasts of more snow during the night kept most Jerusalemites snugly at home. Nevertheless, by eight P.M. some forty feminists had braved the weather to gather in a plush apartment near the Prime Minister's House to debate the political future of the feminist movement. The main item on the agenda: whether to run for the Knesset elections in May 1977.

The issue had been raised by feminist Member of Knesset Marcia Freedman, a small, soft-voiced philosophy lecturer who had been elected in 1973 as the third representative of the Citizens' Rights Movement, then a new liberal party with three Members of Knesset. On this evening, just over three years later, she declared that she had always considered her mandate a feminist one and that she was offering it to the feminist movement with the following three alternatives: the movement could run independently for Knesset, it could merge with a left-of-center coalition, or it could return the mandate to Freedman to do with as she saw fit. But the movement should decide. Outside it was snowing again, but tension was already too high for anyone to worry about how they would get home.

One group of feminists had already organized politically against electoral action. They had printed a broadside attack which declared: "So what if there's elections in May? . . . Why let an outside event that is not dependent on us dictate our modes of working and thinking? It will destroy the little we've already built, and no one knows what its effect will be on what we want to do, in our own way, in the future." Elections and the feminist effort, they maintained, were worlds apart.

Reaction was sharply emotional. "How can you call elections 'an outside event'?" erupted Shuli, one of the advocates of electoral activity. "Here's a chance to finally get going and have some effect on the public. We'll have a certain amount of money at our disposal from the reelection budget given to a Member of Knesset, an amount of money we've never had before, and this is our only chance to use it. We can't just throw it up!"

"It's a perfect opportunity to get some of our basic points over," seconded Tamar. "It doesn't matter how few votes we get, at least we'll have reached the minds of some women in the country."

Others were more cynical about the chances of communication of a small, new movement working with a minuscule budget compared with that of the larger parties. And they were extremely concerned about the chances of forming a feminist platform within the present reality of Israeli politics.

"What are we going to say about anything other than purely feminist issues?" asked Ofra. "We can't run an election campaign on the issue of abortions."

"Yet we can hardly propose a feminist policy on sewage," added Varda ironically.

The main issue was the need for a clear line on foreign policy and the difficulty of formulating such a line. For example, on the subject of withdrawal from the Israeli-occupied West Bank of the Jordan River, taken from Jordan in the Six Day War of 1967, it was pointed out that two feminists could quite validly argue for contradictory policies—one for moving not an inch, the other for withdrawing from the whole area. Both could invoke the same humanitarian principle of the wish to avoid war, but where one could argue that withdrawal would definitely lead to war, the other could argue that it is no withdrawal that would bring about another war. Both arguments are current in Israel today. The consideration is identical; the conclusions antithetical.

"We can't ignore the reality of the country we live in," argued Leah. "Here voters are concerned first and foremost with war and peace, and I don't see how we can run for elections without relating to this issue. We won't be taken seriously unless we do. And if we can't find a clear and well-argued feminist line, then we can't run for elections."

Despite the desire of many feminists to eschew politics, feminism cannot but be political, since it challenges a fundamental principle of the present social organization of the country. The feminist movement has not defined the direction of its political action since, like nearly all Israel's small parties and political organizations, it is enmeshed in the problems of dogma. But following feminism all the way down the line is a quixotic proposition in a country that does not accept its basic tenets. And far from being ready for the compromises and pragmatic adjustments which entry into Israel's formal political life would entail, the feminist movement reacts in much the same way most small movements do when under attack. It justifies its existence by attempting to purify its philosophy, and in so doing it limits its range and effectiveness.

But this was not the issue that resolved the discussion. The key issue in the decision not to run for elections was membership in the feminist movement. "Listen," said Sara, a devout leftist, "if we run for Knesset we contravene one of our most basic principles, and that's that any woman, no matter what her political beliefs, can join our movement. By running against established political parties, we'd automatically exclude women belonging to or voting for those parties. And what kind of sisterhood is that?" This concentration on membership in the feminist movement as opposed to identification with feminist aims represents a basic flaw in anti-electoral thinking. Increasing membership may stroke the egos of women already in the movement, but it is hardly the most effective means of spreading the feminist philosophy. In a country still striving for femininity, not feminism, feminists must search for alternative paths to women's minds rather than insisting on total commitment to the feminist movement. One path could be the publicity generated by electoral action.

At present, the movement numbers two to five hundred women, depending on whether one counts only active feminists or all those on movement mailing lists. And it is absolutely unacceptable to the Israeli public, women and men. It is often accused of being an American import, partly perhaps because its most public figure, Marcia Freedman, emigrated to Israel from the United States in 1968 and is still regarded as more American than Israeli. The American label can be positive or pejorative in Israel, depending on the context; somehow it is never neutral. Where feminists are concerned, it is pejorative, and is intended to demonstrate that feminist tactics born in the United States cannot succeed in the different reality of Israeli society. Nevertheless, Israelis have adopted the full slew of labels and images imposed on American feminists in the late sixties and transferred them *in toto* to Israeli feminists. While it is argued that feminism cannot survive cultural transplantation, the stereotype apparently can. Thus Israel's feminists are rumored to be ugly, frustrated bra-burners who are taking out their bitterness on society because they cannot be real women.

Such an atmosphere militates strongly against an electoral campaign. Yet so long as Israel's feminists attempt to remain apolitical, Israeli politicians have no need to consider feminism a force to be reckoned with or even taken into account. Major parties declare equal rights for women, but under close questioning are willing to do very little to support their declarations. In the absence of an effective challenge, there is little they need do. And unless they consider any means in order to get through to Israelis at every level, the feminists risk remaining an enclave of well-educated upper-middle-class Israeli women talking more to each other than to other women.

Many feminists are bewildered by the very idea of breaking out of their own social circles to speak to the majority of Israelis. "Here we are raising our consciousness," said a production assistant at Israel Television, "and just look at what's really happening out there!" She had been interviewing a few of those women somewhat quaintly but accurately known as *nashim bemetsuka*, women in distress—mainly Oriental women at a loss as to how to function in a modernizing society. "What on earth can we do for them?" she asked. "Where do we even start? The bread-and-butter problems they face—we don't have them, we don't even understand them, and we're as helpless as they are when it comes to tackling them!" She and others are painfully aware that however far they progress personally, they have not to go far beyond their doorsteps to find their newfound liberation limited by an inability to cope with the large-scale problems of Israeli women. They face the problem of translating belief into effective action that can affect and direct the mainstream of their society—a mainstream from which they feel cut off by their feminist consciousness. Until they solve this dilemma, their chances of building feminism into an effective challenge to femininity are severely limited.

With this awareness, a small group of women decided to appeal to the Israeli public directly by going ahead with a political campaign without the support of the feminist movement. They formed the Women's Party to run for the May 1977 elections. The party's platform was the envy of feminists abroad. It was sexual politics in the most direct sense of the term. For the first time ever, such issues as women's sexuality, recognition of housewives as professional workers, rape and prostitution were central planks in a political campaign platform, alongside issues of women's education, work status and health. Ideologically, it was close to being a perfect feminist platform. But it was hardly calculated to attract votes in the Israel of today. The brief resolution of the foreign policy issue, on which the party took a clear dovish stance, cost them much potential support: "We support any effort towards a solution of the Israel-Arab conflict, including recognition of the rights of the Palestinian people to self-determination and insurance of Israel's security and right to exist. We see Arab women both within the State of Israel and outside it as sisters in our joint struggle for equal rights and opportunities, and look forward to the day when we can shake hands over political borders."

"We needed only two percent of all women's votes to get just one seat in the Knesset," said Marcia Freedman, the éminence grise of the party who did not stand for reelection herself. They got just over half a percent.

The Women's Party's fate was an indication of the distance between feminists and other Israeli women, a distance increased by fear. The more the feminists place themselves apart from the mainstream in their search for ideological purity, the more threatening they become. The feminist philosophy in fact presents a double threat to the majority of Israeli women: it threatens both the feminine norm and the attainment of that norm. For the flight of Israeli women into femininity is still in progress. And as long as the feminine mystique is an aim rather than an achieved fact, feminism challenges aspiration as well as achievement.

The "real woman" myth is a relatively new development in Israel, and the majority of women are still in active pursuit of it. While women in the West have long since gained the plateau of the feminine mystique, Israeli women are still climbing the slopes and gullies to that plateau, and have placed all their hopes on reaching it. Paradoxically, they have more to lose than those who have achieved the full flower of femininity. Once this goal has been attained, women can assess their femininity for what it is worth and direct their hopes elsewhere. But for Israeli women, feminism challenges not just their achievements so far, but also their hopes for the future.

To threaten the intangibles of hope and aspiration is to strike at the structures of life, to rob it suddenly of direction. Israeli women cling to their myths all the more fiercely in the face of feminism because these myths are the road signs of their lives, providing direction and meaning and above all the security of knowing what to expect and what is expected of them. While traveling the highway to femininity, it takes courage to assess the point of arrival and, if it is found wanting, to turn off the highway in search of a new destination. Feminism demands that women consider whether they are on the road by choice or by force of circumstance rationalized as choice. It does not dictate any one direction for women's lives. But it does demand that whatever direction a woman takes, she take it freely. If she chooses to be a full-time housewife and mother, this is a valid choice if it is a real one—that is, if she had real alternatives from which to choose. When only one option is open, for whatever reasons, there is no element of choice. And the danger in Israeli society is that possibilities other than femininity are gradually being withdrawn.

Interestingly, the first steps toward practical feminism are being taken by women who declare themselves nonfeminist. Member of Knesset Shulamit Aloni, a lawyer with an unruly mop of curly hair and a sharp, antagonistic manner, who left the Labor Party and started her own party when Golda Meir became Prime Minister, is an insistent and outspoken fighter for women's rights. She sees this as an integral part of her battle for full civic and civil rights in Israel, and as part of her long and bitter struggle against the religious monopoly on matters of marriage and divorce. She declares herself a non-feminist as much for political as for ideological reasons: to be so dubbed in Israel is the kiss of political death. It was Aloni who asked Marcia Freedman to join the Knesset list of her Citizens' Rights Movement in 1973, bringing Freedman into the parliament, and it is she who has been, over the years, most insistent in proposing a civil marriage bill, a subject the feminists have all but ignored. Feminist inaction on this issue is due partly to inertia and partly to ideological absolutism. Since some feminists are against marriage as an institution, they argue that there is no point in fighting for civil marriage. It is a self-centered and blinkered attitude to maintain in the face of reality.

Aloni's latest attempt was in 1976, when she initiated a

civil marriage bill which was never voted on. The National Religious Party threatened to resign from the coalition and thus bring down the government if the bill was presented for a vote. Much the same fate befell her 1975 bill proposing a "Basic Law: Women's Rights," which stated simply that "There will be full and absolute equality of women in the life of the state, the society and the economy and throughout the whole legislative system, and women will be entitled to every right and to every legal action. Any law which contradicts or will contradict this law is declared null and void." In the explanatory appendix to this proposal, Aloni emphasized that this would entail civil marriage and divorce, and a complete revision of women's status in work, taxes and social welfare. In effect, it was a revolutionary proposal, since it would have meant a thoroughgoing revision of principles throughout Israel's national institutions. The proposal was passed for discussion by the Knesset to the relevant committee, headed by a National Religious Party representative—and there it stayed, deadlocked. As in the case of her 1975 bill, the rapprochement between the theopolitic and the secular politic was once more preserved at the expense of women.

The brick wall that Aloni has charged time and again is known alternatively as the status quo and by the catch-all term *ahdut ha'am,* "unity of the people." This phrase appeals to nationalism as a means of avoiding the *kulturkampf* that is feared if there were to be an outright confrontation between synagogue and state. It is also bandied about in times of crisis to rationalize the demand for a wall-to-wall coalition government of right and left parties. It purports to place national interests above party interests—and places both above women's interests. Even those who, in principle, might agree that the rabbinical courts' monopoly on marriage and divorce should be abolished, hang back from confrontation by hiding behind *ahdut ha'am.*

The latest in the long line of politicians to take this tack is Yigael Yadin, the archeology professor and general turned politician who formed the right-of-center Democratic Movement party to contest the leadership in the 1977 elections. His platform included, as did the Labor Party platform, full and equal rights for women. When asked whether he would change the rabbinical courts' system to achieve this objective, he evaded the issue, saying, "We decided not to have a supermarket of ideas that we will not be able to implement. ... We want to unify the people in this most difficult time, and there are priorities in such situations. When you are in danger, you cannot solve all the problems. And if you think that unity is one of the most important elements, you should strive for the moment not to divide the people on issues that everyone should decide according to his own conscience."[1] The fact that under the law no one has the opportunity to decide according to conscience on this issue is hidden behind the argument of unity in the face of the enemy. This unwillingness to challenge the religious externals of Judaism is the more striking when one remembers that it was Yadin who led the excavation of Massada, the desert stronghold in which Jews held out to the last against Roman conquest, and which provided Jews with an alternative to religion in the form of a strong and tangible historical link with the political and cultural past of Jews in the land of Israel.

Such attitudes are as common on the left as on the right, though differently expressed. Mathematics professor Shaul Fogel, one of the leading figures in a left-wing ideological group called *Shalom Achshav*, Peace Now, is ideologically committed to sexual equality, but it raises problems for him in practice. In a joint meeting of *Shalom Achshav* and a feminist group, he asked whether the leftists should raise the issue of women's status in their contacts with left-wing Palestinians on the West Bank. These are men whose socialism does not include feminism; despite their socialist ideology, they are deeply grounded in the extreme sexism of Arab society. "Equality of the sexes is a subject that can only cause great divisiveness between us," said Fogel, "and yet it is part of our group's ideology. So I ask in all seriousness—I really don't know the answer—should we raise the issue of the status of Arab women with them when it may disrupt everything else we have built up in the way of contact and mutual understanding?"[2] The

feminist answer was that this mutual understanding would re-
dound to the sole benefit of the men on each side if the status
of women was ignored, and that the left was using the same
tactics as the right in avoiding divisiveness at women's expense. Despite his avowal of confusion, women take second
place to male unity for Shaul Fogel, and his thinking reflects
the prevalent feeling throughout Israel's splintered left, including Rakah, the Communist party. The pervasive influence
of the security situation blocks any realistic consideration of
feminism.

Even those whose work has led them to the threshold of
feminism disavow the large-scale import of their efforts. M. K.
Tamar Eshel, head of *Naamat* (the working women's organization affiliated with the Histadrut trade union federation),
acknowledges that the legal force of religious laws with regard
to personal status is a bad blow for women. But, she argues,
"should we demand far-reaching changes at this time, at
the price of splitting the nation when we are involved in a
national struggle for our existence? Are these the only problems we have—making possible the full participation of women
in all fields of human activity in Israel?"[3] Her answer, a shocking one for a women's leader, is that this is not the time to demand change—a refusal that signifies not a lack of theoretical
desire to see real change accomplished, but awe at its scope
and its implications for Israeli society as a whole.

How serious the split within the nation would be is a
moot point. One research survey conducted in 1975, a year
after the eruption of the scandal surrounding the blacklists of
"unmarriageables" kept by the Ministry of Religious Affairs
and the rabbinical courts, indicated that the majority of the
Israeli public is solidly in favor of instituting civil marriage.
Sixty-three percent favored the proposal of a civil marriage
law in the Knesset, and thirty-seven percent opposed it.[4] Moreover, there were indications that the number of those in favor
would be higher were it not that many feared the government
breakdown that would occur if it were seriously initiated and
the National Religious Party left the coalition. Shulamit Aloni

claims that the majority of Knesset members, if they were allowed a free vote on the subject, would vote for a civil marriage bill. How serious, in that case, would the split within
the nation be? Indications are that such a move would be
welcome to the majority of Israelis. But no move is made. It
is often argued that the presence of the National Religious
Party within the coalition government is the power-politic
block to such a move; but no government attempt was made to
advance a civil marriage law even when the N.R.P. was not in
the coalition, for example, during the first few months of the
Rabin government in 1974.

Here too there is a deep confusion within Israeli minds
between what is desirable and what should be effected. Israel
is not yet ready to fight "the war of the Jews" over what it
means to be a Jew, partly because that war could be very
violent. The small but fanatic population of ultra-Orthodox
Jews have bloodied the heads of other Israelis over such issues
as driving on the Sabbath and performing autopsies. On the
issue of civil marriage they might erupt in full-scale riots.
There is no public pressure to initiate such a war, and political pressure in the Knesset is limited to the few who are willing to act on their principles. Until there is a concerted effort by those most directly interested in civil marriage—Israeli
women—it seems unlikely that civil marriage would be intro-
duced and women released from the religious laws of property
even were the National Religious Party to remain permanently
outside the government.

Far from being outside the government, however, the
N.R.P. now enjoys greater power than ever before. In June
1977, Premier Menahem Begin formed a coalition of his right-
wing Likud party with the N.R.P. and the ultra-Orthodox
Agudath Israel party. To many, the specter of a theocracy had
become a reality.

It was a logical coalition, despite the N.R.P.'s former
"historic partnership" with Labor. Likud and N.R.P. sup-
porters had already united in the messianic nationalist *Gush
Emunim* movement, created to encourage Jewish settlement in

the occupied West Bank of the Jordan River by fair means or foul. Where the followers had already united, the leaders now did so too.

Perhaps the best indication of what awaits Israeli women under the Likud coalition is found in the actual coalition agreement signed by the Likud and Agudath Israel, in which the three main points were: repeal of the abortion law reform; easier procedures for women to avoid army service by declaring themselves religious; and definition of "who is a Jew" for purposes of citizenship according to the strictest definition of *halacha*. But still more disturbing than the points themselves is the fact that the Likud made no compromise in assenting to these Agudath Israel demands. There was no conflict of interest or principles, for all three points reflect the prevailing feeling in the Likud, if not its declared policy.

But even before the Likud came to power, the unwillingness to broach the possibility of civil marriage and the fear of confrontation on the issue was reflected in a forum that should have placed it among its top priorities: the Prime Minister's Commission on the Status of Women. Declared as a gesture to International Women's Year, the commission was actually established a year later, partly due to feminist pressure. It agreed not to recommend anything on the civil marriage issue, restricting itself to discussing minor changes in *halacha* (rabbinical law), which are unlikely to be implemented. The reason for this avoidance of a major issue was indicated by the commission's chairwoman, Labor Member of Knesset Ora Namir, who describes herself as "a pragmatist" and therefore confined both herself and the commission to those issues which stand at least a chance of solution within the present reality of Israeli society and its legislation. But by accepting the status quo the commission absolved itself of any responsibility for changing it.

Nevertheless, the commission did commit itself on many issues within the confines established by Ora Namir. Her voice, soft but firm and controlled, set the tone for the commission as a whole. Its recommendations range from unqualified advocacy of nationally available family planning services to various proposals for ensuring fuller participation of women in the economy and society. Although on civil marriage it was powerless, and on many other issues equivocal, the commission placed great stress on equality for women at work and better job training for women, and also on services which will allow women to join the work force—in particular, day nurseries and a longer school day (to four in the afternoon instead of the present midday). These are radical steps in Israel, and there is little chance of their being adopted unless the commission continues as an ad hoc pressure group lest its recommendations fall by the wayside—a fate most likely under the former Labor government, but practically certain under the Likud.

But such issues, though vital, are symptomatic rather than causative. Ora Namir touches the root of the problem when she talks of the indifference of Israeli women to issues which concern them directly. Resignation to the family role underlies this indifference and accounts for what Namir, a long-time socialist, calls the "regression" of Israeli women out of their society and into their homes.[5]

In the long run, the main import of the commission may lie less in its recommendations than in the dynamics of its working progress. The commission brought most of Israel's leading women academicians, politicians and administrators into a joint working framework for the first time. They found themselves breaking through lines of personal, political and historical antipathy. As the statistical picture of the status of Israeli women became clearer, many went through a gradual process of what can only be called consciousness-raising, though they themselves would deny it. This was reflected as early as the interim report, published at the end of 1976. In the Introduction to this report Ora Namir gave a well-deserved retort to Premier Rabin's opening sentence in his Knesset speech declaring his intention to establish the commission.[6] "It is fitting that the Knesset take time off from its regular business ... to pay tribute to the Israeli woman," said Rabin. One and a half years later Ora Namir replied, "One principle in the Commission's work is clear and beyond doubt, and that is that the status of Israeli women is not an abstract value which can be dealt with in "spare time." . . . The status of women is one of the basic values of the state."[7]

Like many other members of the commission, Namir does not see herself as a feminist, but she is now talking feminism. The working friendships and partnerships within the commission developed over a year's research into a situation far worse than many of its members had imagined when they began working, and have created a certain solidarity and a desire to see the recommendations put into effect and not used merely for public relations purposes. Whether the commission members will be able to maintain this newfound solidarity is another question. In 1974 Marcia Freedman, then a fledgling member of the Eighth Knesset, attempted to form a women's caucus of all women Members of Knesset, across party lines, and met with blunt refusal. The chances of forming such a caucus today are better due to the fact that the majority of women Knesset members served together on the commission. But a formal attempt would probably still be doomed because party lines are too strict. A de facto caucus on certain issues might be possible; it depends on the will, and the loyalties, of the women concerned.

The commission is not the only sign of progress in the last two or three years. Many small changes have taken place. Perhaps the most significant of these is the fact that a woman is now training as an air force pilot. A new immigrant from France, she had been flying for ten years before she came to Israel in 1975 and insisted that she be allowed to fly in the air force. The course is still in progress, and it is as yet unclear whether she will complete it (the drop-out rate is extremely high) or what her task in the air force will be if she does. But the fact that she has broken the ban on women training as air force pilots may be a sign of a breakthrough in military thinking.

Other changes involve more people on a lesser level. In journalism, *At,* a major women's magazine published once a month, has taken a relatively feminist tone, with a new intelligence and respect for its readers in discussion of both women's and general issues. Women journalists from the daily press have in some instances begun an about-face in their attitudes toward other women. While some are beyond hope, such as *Yediot Aharanot's* Hadassah Mor, who maintains that in the majority of wife-beating cases it is the wife who provokes the husband into beating her, others, such as *Maariv's* Tamar Avidar, who once wrote coy and salable illustrated books on such subjects as "How to keep your husband," have changed over to responsible, intelligent reporting.

Television journalists are also beginning to change. The main message of a two-hour program discussing divorce, in December 1976, though it was never stated in so many words, was women's liberation—specifically the need for women to get out of the house and create an interesting and independent life for themselves, alongside their family lives. One particularly strong personality who appeared on the program was a happy, attractive and well-adjusted divorcee, Nili Arnon. At nineteen she had married because she was pregnant. "I really wanted to be an ideal wife," she recalled, "and an ideal wife is one who stays home and looks after her husband. . . . I tried to be part of him, to see the world through his eyes. I thought he was the one who would bring the world to me. . . . But the more I tried, the worse I felt. It got to where I felt helpless, that I'd missed my chance in life. . . . I couldn't see myself divorced, couldn't even conceive of it. . . . I rejected the idea because I was so scared of it." Finally, however, divorce became a positive alternative to her marriage, and she broke out. "Now I have the feeling that many women I know envy me, they envy my courage and the life I lead now," she said smiling a little sadly.[8] She and some of the other women who appeared on the program were, in effect, positive role models, presenting alternatives to the accepted role of women in Israel.

There have also been changes in the established women's organizations, which had fought radically for women's rights before the establishment of the State but then fell back into relative insignificance. WIZO (Women's International Zionist Organization) was strong enough to run as a party for the First Knesset and get one woman elected, but since then has concentrated on the traditionally female spheres of charity and welfare. It has now begun to rediscover its political feet and has discussed whether to run once again for the Knesset as a separate list, though it eventually decided against. The Working Women's Council changed both its name (to *Naamat*) and some of its tactics in 1976, taking a more activist tone in its publications and activities. It initiated discussion groups for women in development towns which were consciousness-raising on a basic level, and it published a survey of leading politicians' answers to specific questions on women's issues in one issue of its magazine. The questions were more impressive than the answers.

Such changes reflect, in part, the spread of feminism in the West, which reaches Israel through the filter of mass circulation magazines, avidly read by English-speaking Israelis, and through contacts of those who are affluent enough to travel or even live abroad. While they may reject their native feminists, elite women are not unimpressed by the relative respectability and acceptance of feminism in the West. They argue that the American style of feminism is not acceptable in Israel, and many still claim that there is no need for feminism in Israel, but the thinking of some is slowly changing.

Perhaps one of the major factors in this new willingness to start thinking along more activist lines was the Yom Kippur War of 1973. While the traumatic effect of that war for Israel provided a verbal playground for journalists, psychologists and politicians alike, few paused to consider its effect on Israeli women. The pattern of Israeli sex typing and stereotyping is emphasized in wartime, a phenomenon which is hardly surprising in a society which lays such stress on security and tends to balance national security with security in the home. Far from breaking the conservative pattern of sex roles, Israeli's wars have strengthened them. It is in wartime, when they are most enclosed in their feminine role, that Israeli women feel its full burden. The Yom Kippur War, because of its length, the pain of surprise attack, and its apparent futility, brought out these feelings more clearly than ever. Israel was desperately and bravely fighting for its life against numerically superior forces who had the advantage of the initiative, and women were allowed no part in this effort. They were not called into the army reserves, since they were wives and mothers; and when they attempted to volunteer for such duties as mail, bread and milk deliveries on the home front, their teenage children were accepted instead. They were told, "We don't need women," or "Lady, go home and look after your children. Leave it all to us."

The frustration of inaction and the realization of being alloted no job in a society totally directed to the war effort created a vast pool of guilt. Most women sat at home in the knowledge that others were dying for them. They worried and gossiped, and horror-tale rumors quickly spread to feed their anxiety. Many attempted to convert their guilt into action through the classically feminine activities left open to them: baking cakes for "the boys at the front," knitting balaclavas for soldiers on the snowbound Golan Heights, and listening, listening all the time, to the news bulletins, trying to find out what was going on. The three weeks of the Yom Kippur War and the months of high alert that followed it demanded the maximum of every man and the minimum of women.

Psychologist Tamar Breznitz-Svidovsky has described the main focus of Israeli women's wartime activity as "nest-building"[9]—the small attentions to the home, the baking, sewing, embroidering and knitting by which Israeli women lined the nest against the rainy day that had already arrived. But their helplessness was palpable. For what seemed a shockingly large number, it extended to an inability to handle the minor technicalities of everyday life—paying bills, writing checks, changing light bulbs—things their husbands had always handled. In their absence, the wives now realized to what extent protection had created the inability to cope.

Within a year of that war, the trauma had been largely absorbed and relegated to the national subconscious, desensitized by military and political analysis, and shelved neatly as "lessons learned." Women swallowed their frustration and guilt, and again accepted their role as vulnerable and protected. Until the next time. When the national bus company,

Egged, finally announced in 1974 that it would run courses for
women drivers in times of emergency, only a few women en-
rolled, and even fewer completed the courses.

The record of women's feelings during those months is
stored away in the archives of Israel's newspapers, and the
small flurry of women's-page articles expressing women's feelings at the time are long forgotten. One of the most poignant
of these articles was an interview with theater director Nola
Chilton, a member of Kibbutz Shamir on the Mediterranean
coast. She set down some of the feeling of the time in her
documentary *Women in War*, a play which developed out
of her own sense of helplessness during and after the Yom
Kippur War. "I asked myself, what am I? A parasite? It was
a terrible feeling of impotence. I felt small and alone, even
though I was in a kibbutz, surrounded by hundreds of women."
Her husband and son were in the army, "And I sat at home
and didn't know what to do. Terrible, terrible!"[10]

Few women can live with that sense of the terrible for long,
and fewer can act on it. A small number of the elite are
becoming more aware of the problems facing Israeli women,
and a still smaller number are attempting to act. But the
majority still take their situation for granted, invoking the
idols of nature and security to rationalize their role. They
remain, and choose to remain, oblivious to the possibilities of
sexual equality, placing what they see as national and natural
interests above their personal ones, and confining their energy
and vitality largely to the home.

What can happen when this vitality wins through and an
Israeli woman places her own interests above other considera-
tions, even those of security, is personified by a woman who is
neither a leader nor a politician, but an athlete. Esther
Shahamarov-Roth saw her coach and most of her teammates
slaughtered by Palestinian terrorists in the 1972 Olympics at
Munich. She returned to hurdling with a grit and determination that brought her to the finals of the 1976 Montreal
Olympics, breaking her own record three times in the process.
Roth's mode of dealing with the security problem, which had
affected her directly and shatteringly, was neither resignation

nor withdrawal. "Munich is something one never forgets," she says today. "It is always there. But that does not mean that one always thinks about it."

Within three months of that terrible experience Roth was back on the track, training. "The pull was too strong to resist," she says. "I still felt I hadn't reached what I could in my field. We left Munich before I could really test myself out on the track, it was unfinished work for me, and I had to go on and try and reach what I felt was my potential." In 1976, just twenty months after giving birth by Caesarean section, Roth bore all Israeli's hopes and fears on her shoulders as she ran in Montreal. "I gave all those interviews at the time as an Israeli, not as an athlete," she remembers. "For an athlete, it's the worst thing that could happen, being reminded all the time of Munich by reporters, of all those people at home depending on me. Yet I felt I couldn't refuse." The blend of strength and vulnerability that she projected in those press and television interviews, and her lack of self-pity as she concentrated on her purpose, expressed all that Israeli women are capable of being: strong not as suffering mothers or widows but as people determined to deal with and act in the world; vulnerable not as weak women but as people capable of feeling and remembering without allowing those feelings and memories to control their everyday lives.

This is the real political challenge. The most fundamental kind of political change that Israeli women can undergo is psychological change—a change in the way they deal with the realities of their country's security and other problems, an about-face from self-sacrifice and withdrawal for the collective good to placing individual ambition and fulfillment first. The collective and the individual good stand in no opposition to each other here, for by becoming independent, active individuals Israeli women will contribute immeasurably, as did Esther Roth, to their country.

While women such as Shulamit Aloni advocate legal-political change, sociologists such as Rivka Bar-Yosef advocate more women in decision-making positions, the feminists advocate revolution, and politicians such as Ora Namir con-

centrate on the problems of getting women out of the home
and into the work force, all really ignore the fundamental
process that must underpin success or failure in their efforts
—the need for psychological change. The political challenge
is first and foremost a psychological one.

It is one that affects the whole of Israel, and that relates
deeply to Israel's security problem. It involves a confrontation
with what might be described as Israel's *Report from Iron
Mountain* mentality,* where in a sense it is as well that the
security issue continues to "unite the people" lest other issues,
such as women's status, rise to the top and erupt. In a country
where 40 percent of the national budget is spent directly on
defense and close to another 30 percent goes to defense-related
loans, and where defense spending per capita is three times as
high as in the United States despite an average income that
is less than a third as great, security is a major issue to confront. But it involves more than defense spending, wartime
activity, women's service in the army, and the like. It involves
Israel's existential sense of security in all realms: security in its
Jewishness, security in its existence and its ability to continue
to exist, and above all security in its future—the ability to
take for granted what is taken for granted elsewhere. It involves the basic issues of national, spiritual and personal life
and death.

There is no doubt that a number of practical devices will
improve the status of Israeli women: devices to help them out
into the work force, and to provide options of family planning,
better education and training, and legal aid and legal protection of their rights as equals. A major step would be the aboli-
tion of the theopolitic—not just the rabbinical courts'

---

* *Report from Iron Mountain on the Possibility and Desirability of
Peace* (Leonard L. Lewin, ed.; Delta, 1967) is the hypothetical
report of a top-level U.S. government commission convened to
explore the consequences of lasting peace on American society. It
concluded that war serves important stabilizing functions in society,
and that the country's economy, social structure and psychology
would be seriously undermined by lasting peace, since no alternative stabilizing systems have been developed.

monopoly on marriage and divorce but the stranglehold of the National Religious Party, a major factor in both sexual and national chauvinism in Israel and a force diametrically opposed to any territorial concession on the West Bank. As long as it holds the balance of power inside Israel, the National Religious Party can veto any major advance toward peace in the Middle East and ensure that the present insecurity of Israel's security situation continue. If the distinction can be drawn between religion and politics, faith and imposition, belief and dogmatism, choice and resignation, then the cause of both Israeli women and peace will have been advanced. How far that advance will reach, however, depends on the psychological readiness for change.

"Those who can face the challenge of a truth and build their lives to accord are finally not many, but the very few," wrote Joseph Campbell,[11] discussing the need for myths. There are some few Israeli women who are attempting to challenge the myths behind which their sisters hide. But a total challenge to femininity, its yokes, cults and panaceas, still seems overwhelming when it means questioning myths by which the society lives.

Yet it must be attempted, or the myths will obliterate the question of what the society lives *for*, fixating it at a level far below its potential. In the final analysis, no matter how many the reforms squeezed through in concession to ideology, it may well be that Israeli women will not escape the limitations of femininity nor be ready to demand and enjoy full equality until there is some form of peace for Israel. But lest that peace be meaningless for them, they must start now.

Epilogue—To Israeli Women

I have long since lost count of how many times I have driven out of Jerusalem to research this book. But each of those many times, I took the main road out of the city—the four-laned highway that hugs the sides of the Judean Hills as it bends, rises and dips through the mountains to the coastal plain below. The lower part of this road is Shaar Hagai, a deep cut into the foothills which is flanked by monuments. At the top a sculpture of huge steel shards points toward Jerusalem, symbolizing for many the thrust of Israeli forces to break through the Arab siege of the city in the 1948 War of Independence. Along the route lie the wrecks of armored cars that took part in that near-suicidal attempt and were hit by enemy guns perched high on the mountain slopes overlooking the road; they have been painted rust color in anti-rust paint and left by the new roadside.

After that war Shaar Hagai was intensively planted. The stones and thorns of the Judean Hills disappeared under hundreds of thousands of young Jerusalem pines, crowding the steep slopes down to the very verge of the road itself. But that was not to be the end of death in Shaar Hagai.

In 1974 the trees of Shaar Hagai began dying of a mysterious disease that could not be identified. It was a strange death. It took just the Jerusalem pines, not the other trees and bushes that had come to life on the reforested slopes, and it took them from the inside out. While the trunks and inner

206

branches of the pines were gray with death, the outer branches were still green. But each time I drove past, it seemed as if the gray had crept farther along the branches toward the outside; and so it was.

For years, what appeared to be life to the casual passer-by —the mass of verdure greeting the eye as one drove round another bend in the road—was just a mask. It was only on close inspection, on wandering through the forest itself, that one could see the extent of the damage and touch the tragedy that was quietly overtaking the forest.

The tragedy of Shaar Hagai was more than love of nature and the death of a forest. It was the death of a symbol. Trees in Israel symbolize fertility. They represent barrenness conquered, life created where before there had been only rocks, rebirth in a hostile climate, and a people reborn out of the stones and thorns of its past. And so a strange mourning took many of us unawares as we made our way up to or down from Jerusalem and saw the trees dying under the glare of the sun.

I still remember the acute pain I felt when the foresters cut down the first of the dead trees. They had held off for as long as they could, hoping that a solution could be found. But as acre after planted acre gave way to the disease, and expert after expert threw up his hands in helplessness, the decision was finally taken to clear away the affected trees and to replant.

That was in the fall of 1975. The winter rains followed. They were still clearing the forest and had not yet started replanting. And then the spring of 1976 brought a new sight. There where the dead pines had been cut down, fresh green was emerging. The bushes and trees that had been hidden from sight by the pines, exposed for the first time in years to the sunlight, were steadily growing upward through the rocks. There were masses of green among the gray layers of cut pines waiting to be carried down the slopes; the vast undergrowth of the forest was coming into its own under the searchlight of the spring and summer sun.

All this was happening as I was pondering and researching this book, and the new growth gave me comfort. In the

death and rebirth of the Shaar Hagai forest I saw a hopeful
parallel to the future of Israeli women. As the foresters were
chopping through the dead cover of diseased pines to expose
the healthy undergrowth beneath, I thought perhaps I could
chop a little way through the deadened cover of myths and
ideologies by which Israeli women lead their everyday lives,
perhaps reach the strength and vitality that lies beneath,
ignored and untended.

I talked to hundreds of women and went through an often
painful rethinking and reappraisal as I wrote this book. I am
convinced that a healthy alternative is achievable within, and
even despite, the realities of Israeli society today.

At the beginning of 1977 I began to organize a non-
partisan women's list to run for the Jerusalem city council and
try to get a block of at least four or five women elected.*
I approached women from all walks of life—poor women from
the *schunot* (Jerusalem's slum and semi-slum neighborhoods),
professional women, and rich women from the affluent neighborhoods. Their interest and response led me to believe that
this was an idea whose time perhaps had come. If approached
and asked to do so, women were apparently ready to start
acting in their own interests, to emerge from their cover and
enjoy a growing realization that together they could create
and exert control over the everyday conditions of their own
lives.

I had been convinced of the underlying strength and
vitality of Israeli women, and this conviction was borne out
by the response. I had always thought of Theodor Herzl's
words when he envisaged the creation of a Jewish state—
"If you will it, it is no dream"—as an outworn cliché. Now
these words suddenly seemed relevant. If the will of Israeli
women can be aroused and if they can find conviction in their
ability, they can demand and take their equal place in Israeli
society.

These are big ifs but vital ones for any change in either
men's attitudes toward women or women's attitudes toward

---

* The municipal elections were eventually postponed until 1978.

themselves. Israel's extreme male orientation and the paternalism of its leadership's view of women make it easy for Israeli men to assume—since little is ever claimed to the contrary—that their life experiences have no relevance for women and that women are determined more by their biology than by their experience. It rarely occurs to an Israeli man that his norms and values affect women as strongly as they affect him, although in a very different direction.

But what is more disturbing is the fact that women have rarely troubled to point out this fact. On Friday night, the Sabbath eve, people all over Israel sit back comfortably after a satisfying meal, sip coffee and crack sunflower seeds, watch television or talk and smoke until everyone runs out of cigarettes and the evening breaks up. I have spent many such evenings deep in discussion of male and female roles, with the men arguing for retention of the traditionally feminine role while the women sat back and generally kept silent. Maybe they would smile knowingly or mysteriously, nod their heads here and there, perhaps glance with fond forgiveness at their male partners for their shortsightedness and egocentricity. But few women would speak their minds in such gatherings. When they did, it was often to agree with the men. And on those rare occasions when it was to disagree, it seemed to me that they regretted their words, that they wanted to avoid opening a Pandora's box of contention and confrontation.

The next day, or the day after, I might speak with them on the telephone or meet them by chance in the street, as happens in Jerusalem, and as happened with Dalia, a social worker, one Sunday.

"You know, you're right," she told me. "It's important, what you say, and it's about time it came out."

"But then why didn't you say anything yourself?" I asked in amazement.

She smiled at me indulgently, almost the same smile she had given her husband that Friday night. "Listen, for you it's safe," she said. "You're free of this society, part of it and yet apart from it, an Israeli citizen but not Israeli-born. You can enter or leave this society as you like, stand outside it or come in and participate. You have the option, and we who were born here don't. We have to live with this society for the rest of our lives, like it or not. We don't have your choice, and therefore our stake is greater. We have more to lose, in fact. You, you're in a position where you can take the risk for us."

Of course Dalia is right. I do have the choice. But the very fact of having made that choice and in effect constantly remaking it by living in Israel, makes my commitment to and involvement in the country very deep. It is true, however, that I do not risk the basis on which I build my life by examining the paradoxes and contradictions of women's status in Israeli society.

The truth is that if I had been born in Israel, I do not know if I would have written this book. Sometimes I like to think I would have, but at others I fear that if I had been subjected to the major influences on Israeli women's lives throughout my childhood, I would have been unable to write about them at this stage in Israel's history. My childhood was a very different one. I was never fed the illusion that I was liberated, and therefore never had to rationalize my evident nonliberation. I lived in the relative security of post-Second World War England, a country which has been under no physical threat to its survival since the year I was born. And although I was raised under the third major influence that affects Israeli women, Judaism, it remained merely a religion that had nothing to offer me until my arrival in Israel. It was then that I made contact with and started feeling, for the first time, the depths of the Jewish tradition—not just its religion, but its history, its tragedy, its values, and above all its attitudes toward women.

It took many years before I was able to grapple with the triad that governs the lives of Israeli women, the triad of liberation, security and religion. I had to pass through stages of amazement, incomprehension and accusation before I could see the force and dynamics of these influences and achieve even a small degree of dispassionate analysis. It was a hard-won understanding, and one that convinced me that until we women in Israel confront the myth of our liberation, the power of religious tradition, and the effects of our national security/insecurity, we resign ourselves to the roles assigned us by a male-oriented society.

This resignation is a defense mechanism. By persuading ourselves that now is not the time to confront the issues, we avoid the pain of realization. We also surrender the right to be equal citizens. "Resignation is only abdication and flight," Simone de Beauvoir wrote in *The Second Sex*. It is a way to avoid not only confrontation, but also the basic problem of deciding for ourselves the lives we wish to live.

The decision to confront the reality of our lives is no small step. It involves breaking through the web of contradictions that forces us into a superficial femininity and binds us into the myths of nature and womanhood; and it means challenging the norms of a society which, through tragic exigency and traditional sanctity, has raised masculinity to its highest value. The strength of the defender of wife and home, the male honor and machismo of the Middle East and North Africa, the patriarchal nature of Judaism—these manifestations of sexism are strangling Israeli women as surely as our foremothers were stifled into silence in the ghettos of the Diaspora, and as effectively as women were subdued some five thousand years ago, when a desert tribe found a new and different god—a masculine god—and a new land promised them by that god.

Decision is a painful process for many, one which the majority of us spend our lives avoiding. We persuade ourselves that by not deciding we have in fact made a decision, that we surrender control of our lives of our own free will. We adopt a passive helplessness or a fashionable "openness" by declaring, "That's the way it is, that's life." And we huddle together in the norms of this small, beleaguered country, searching for the consensus that will give us the strength to withstand war after war, the pressures of international politics and financial interests, the bitter experience of seeing lives lost with still no end in sight.

We all treasure the day when there will be peace in the Middle East, and yet I fear it too. I fear that if Israeli women continue to subordinate their identities to the demands of the national security situation, their reaction when that situation is finally solved will be, "My God, is this it? Is this all? Was it really worth it?" The issue is not only survival; it is the quality of survival. For women pay the price of security no less than men: while men lose their lives, women lose their identities.

If war would solve the security situation, it might, as one of the characters in the documentary play *Women in War* says, be worth it: "If we could only know that these small children would have it easier, that they won't have to go through it all again . . ." But we cannot know. And the question thus becomes: How long are we willing to wait? For how long will Israeli women submerge their identities in the single identity imposed by a society at war or anticipating war? And for how long are we willing to postpone the question of the quality of our lives both now and in an eventual peace?

Life beyond biology, beyond the fluttering of a heartbeat or the register of brain waves on graph paper, is what justifies biological existence. Survival alone is not enough; we must start work on the quality of our survival right now. It is time for Israeli women to come out of the shadows and take an active part in shaping their society. I believe that more and more Israeli women are beginning to realize this. For just as the sheer vitality of the Shaar Hagai undergrowth kept it growing all those years beneath the dying pines, so too Israeli women have retained their energy and vitality—and now, perhaps, will be ready to use it.

References

CHAPTER 1. THREE MYTHS

1. Beba Idelson: *The Status of Women on the State's Silver Jubilee*, an article published by the Foreign Ministry in 1973 (in Hebrew).

2. Shulamit Aloni: "The Status of the Woman in Israel," in *Judaism*, Spring 1973.

3. Rachel: "Perhaps," in Sholom J. Kahn: "The Poetry of Rachel," in *Ariel*, 38, 1975. Translated by Professor Kahn.

4. In Ada Maimon: *Women Build a Land* (Herzl Press, 1962), a history of working women in Israel from 1904 to 1954, packed full of information and insight in a field otherwise all but ignored.

5. Quoted in Ada Maimon, *ibid.*

6. *Ibid.*

7. Golda Meir: *My Life* (Steimatzky, 1975).

8. Ada Maimon, *op. cit.*

9. Yigal Allon: *Shield of David: the story of Israel's armed forces* (Weidenfeld and Nicholson, 1970).

10. David Apter in Introduction to *Ideology and Discontent*, ed. David Apter (Free Press, 1964).

11. One of the most useful sources on statistics concerning Israeli women is *Working Material on the Subject of Women in Israel* (in Hebrew), ed. A. Ofek (Work and Welfare Research Institute, Hebrew University of Jerusalem, 1976), a collection of statistics from various sources on women's status in Israel. In English, sociologist Dorit Padan-Eisenstark wrote two articles full of statis-

tical information: "Are Israeli Women Really Equal?" in *Journal of Marriage and the Family*, 1973, pp. 538–545; and "Image and Reality: Women's Status in Israel," in *Cross-Cultural Perspectives in Women's Status*, ed. R. Leavitt (Mouton, 1974). Also useful is P. Lahav: "The Status of Women in Israel—Myth and Reality," in *The American Journal of Comparative Law*, 24, 1974.

12. "Survey of Income of Employees," in *Monthly Bulletin of Statistics* (in Hebrew) (Central Bureau of Statistics, September 1976).

13. Erik H. Erikson: *Young Man Luther: A Study in Psychoanalysis and History* (Faber and Faber, 1958).

14. In *The Woman in the Kibbutz* (in Hebrew) (Givat Haviva, Kibbutz Research Institute, July 21, 1974).

15. Theodor Herzl: *Old-New Land* (Herzl Press, 1960).

16. Rivka Bar-Yosef and Ilana Shelach: "The Position of Women in Israel," in *Integration and Development in Israel*, ed. S. N. Eisenstadt *et al.* (Israel University Press, 1970).

17. In *Working Material on the Subject of Women in Israel*, *op. cit.*

18. See Rivka Bar-Yosef *et al.*: *Women's Attitudes to Family Life* (in Hebrew) (Hebrew University of Jerusalem, 1973).

19. Shoshana Sharni: *Characteristics of Moroccan and Yemenite Women with 0–8 Years Schooling* (in Hebrew) (Demographic Center, Prime Minister's Office, Jerusalem, 1973).

20. In *Working Material on the Subject of Women in Israel*, *op. cit.*

21. See Clifford Geertz: "Ideology as a Cultural System," in *Ideology and Discontent, op. cit.*

22. The "double bind" theory was first presented by Gregory Bateson *et al.* in "Toward a Theory of Schizophrenia," in *Behavioral Science*, 1, 1956.

23. Betty Friedan: *The Feminine Mystique* (Norton, 1963).

24. Robert Graves: *Mammon and the Black Goddess* (Doubleday, 1965).

25. Naomi Zorea: "Letter to the Daughters of Israel," reprinted in *The Jerusalem Post*, March 11, 1974.

26. Prime Minister Yitzhak Rabin: "Greetings on the Occasion of International Women's Year," speech to the Knesset on February 12, 1975 (Government Press Office Bulletin).

27. Robert Graves, *op. cit.*

28. Dalia Rabikovitz: "The Dove" (Institute for the Translation of Hebrew Literature, Tel Aviv), translated by Dom Moraes.

CHAPTER 2. THE JUDAIC YOKE

1. The "theopolitic" is well described by Norman Zucker in *The Coming Crisis in Israel: Private Faith and Public Policy* (MIT Press, 1973). The implications of political religion are also well delineated in Georges Friedmann's *The End of the Jewish People?* (Doubleday Anchor, 1968), and in Gershon Weiler's *Jewish Theocracy* (in Hebrew) (Am Oved–Ofakim, 1977).

2. Ta'anith, 7a.

3. The English version of the *Shulhan Aruch* is an abridged one: *Code of Jewish Law*, ed. Rabbi Solomon Ganzfried (Hebrew Publishing Company, 1927).

4. P. Lahav: "The Status of Women in Israel—Myth and Reality," in *The American Journal of Comparative Law*, 24, 1974.

5. Rabbi Menahem Hacohen interviewed by Tal Tsabar-Nativ in "League of Women's Rights in the Rabbinical Courts," in *Davar*, September 8, 1975 (in Hebrew).

6. See Rabbi A. I. Unterman: *Family Purity, Its Wide Implications* (Israel Central Committee for Taharas Hamishpacha), a booklet given to all English-speaking couples registering at the Marriage Registry in Israel.

7. Rabbanit Rachel Neria: *Happy Marriage* (in Hebrew) (Israel Central Committee for Taharas Hamishpacha), the Hebrew-language booklet given to couples resgistering to marry.

8. Published in *Yediot Aharonot*, July 8, 1975.

9. Norman Zucker, *op. cit.*

10. Simon N. Herman: *Israelis and Jews, the Continuity of an Identity* (Random House, 1970).

11. Yitzhak Rabin: "Address at a Hebrew University Graduation Ceremony," in *In the Dispersion*, 7, 1967.

12. Zelda: "The Wicked Neighbor," in *Fourteen Israeli Poets: a selection of modern Hebrew poetry*, ed. Dennis Silk (Andre Deutsch, 1976). Translated by Hannah Hoffman.

For general information on women's status under Israeli religious laws, two books by Members of Knesset Shulamit Aloni are excellent: *The Arrangement: from a state of law to a state of halacha* (in Hebrew) (Otpaz, 1970), and *Women as People* (Keter, 1977). Two useful anthologies on Jewish women are "The Jewish Woman, an Anthology" (*Response*, summer 1973), and *The Jewish Woman, New Perspectives*, ed. E. Koltun (Schocken, 1976).

CHAPTER 3. THE CULT OF FERTILITY

1. David Ben-Gurion: "How can the birthrate be increased?" (in Hebrew), in *Ha'aretz*, December 8, 1967.

2. An excellent sourcebook for early Hebrew religions is Raphael Patai's *The Hebrew Goddess* (Ktav, 1967).

3. In Sholom J. Kahn: "The Poetry of Rachel," in *Ariel*, 38, 1975. Translated by Professor Kahn.

4. The term "Isaac syndrome" was coined by criminologist Shlomo Shoham of Tel Aviv University in an address to the International Forum on Adolescence, Jerusalem, July 1976.

5. In *The Seventh Day: soldiers talk about the Six Day War*, ed. Avraham Shapira (English edition edited by Henry Near) (Penguin, 1970).

6. Eliezer Jaffe: "The Jewish Right to Multiply," in *The Jerusalem Post*, September 13, 1976.

7. Amos Kenan: "Artificial Abortion" (in Hebrew) in *Yediot Aharonot*, January 27, 1975.

8. Eliezer Jaffe, *op. cit.*

9. The "Koenig Report," written by Israel Koenig, Chief Commissioner of the Ministry of the Interior for the north of Israel, was leaked to the press. Probably the fullest version was published by *Haolam Hazeh*, September 15, 1976 (in Hebrew).

10. Dov Friedlander: "Population Policy in Israel," in *Population Policy in Developed Countries*, ed. Bernard Berelson (McGraw-Hill, 1974).

11. *Ibid.*

12. Roberto Bachi: *Population Trends of World Jewry* (Institute of Contemporary Jewry, Hebrew University of Jerusalem, 1976).

13. Quoted in Friedlander, *op. cit.*

14. Yeshayahu Leibowitz: "Jewish Identity and Israeli Silence," in *Unease in Zion*, ed. Ehud Ben Ezer (Quadrangle/New York Times, 1974).

15. David Ben Gurion, *op. cit.*

16. Statistics from the *Statistical Abstract of Israel* (Central Bureau of Statistics, Jerusalem, annual) and the *United Nations Demographic Yearbook*.

17. Shlomo Avineri: "Subjugation of the Means to the State's Ends?" in *Unease in Zion, op. cit.*

18. The disparities arise from different statistical methods of estimating the birthrate. Hebrew University demographer Dov Friedlander estimates about 2.6, while the *Statistical Abstract of Israel* estimates 3.12. Most estimates center around the 2.8 mark.

19. Precise estimates differ, but three of the most reliable are in Dov Friedlander: "Family Planning in Israel: Rationality and Ignorance," in *Journal of Marriage and the Family,* February 1973; Roberto Bachi: *Induced Abortions in Israel,* paper presented at the International Conference of the Association for the Study of Abortions, 1968; and Tsiona Peled and Herbert Friedman: *Population Policy in Israel: perceptions and preferences among policy makers, service providers and the public* (American Institute for Research in the Behavioral Sciences, Washington, February 1975).

20. Roberto Bachi: *Induced Abortions in Israel, op. cit.*

21. O. Nadel-Shneor, B. Modan and R. Toaff: "Influence of Selected Demographic Attributes on the Use of Contraceptive Methods" (in Hebrew) in *Harefuah,* April 1, 1971.

22. Dov Friedlander: "Family Planning in Israel: Rationality and Ignorance," *op. cit.*

23. For example in Rivka Bar-Yosef *et al.: Women's Attitudes to Family Life* (in Hebrew) (Hebrew University of Jerusalem, 1973).

24. Tsiona Peled and Herbert Friedman, *op. cit.*

25. Quoted in Augustine Zycher: "The Contraception Case," in *The Jerusalem Post,* April 16, 1976.

26. This shows up clearly in both Tsiona Peled and Herbert Friedman's *Population Policy in Israel* and Rivka Bar-Yosef's *Women's Attitudes to Family Life.*

27. Tsiona Peled and Herbert Friedman, *op. cit.*

28. In Boaz Evron: "More on Problems of Poverty" (in Hebrew) in *Yediot Aharonot,* December 10, 1976.

29. Esther Goshen-Gottstein: *Marriage and First Pregnancy: cultural influences on attitudes of Israeli women* (Tavistock, 1966).

30. Baruch Nadel: "A Women's Discussion in a Slum Neighborhood" (in Hebrew) in *Yediot Aharonot,* June 3, 1976.

31. Robert Graves: *Mammon and the Black Goddess* (Doubleday, 1965).

32. "Golda Talks to Oriana Fallaci," in *Ms.,* April 1973.

33. Golda Meir: *My Life* (Steimatzky, 1975).

CHAPTER 4. ZIONISM AND MANHOOD

1. Edward Leach: *Culture and Communication* (Cambridge University Press, 1976).

2. In Amos Elon's *The Israelis: Founders and Sons,* probably the best and certainly the most readable analysis of Israeli society yet written (Holt, Rinehart and Winston, 1971).

3. Jay Y. Gonen: *A Psycho-History of Zionism* (Meridian, 1976).

4. Haim Hazaz: "The Sermon," in *First Fruits, a harvest of 25 years of Israeli writing,* ed. James A. Michener (Fawcett, 1974).

5. Jay Y. Gonen, *op. cit.*

6. A phrase used by Professor Yadin, as he puts it, in "numerous public lectures on archeology."

7. Arthur Koestler: *Thieves in the Night* (Macmillan, 1946).

8. Herbert Russcol: *The First Million Sabras* (Dodd Mead, 1970).

9. The three potboilers referred to are, respectively: W. A. Ballinger: *The Six-Day Loving* (Mayflower, 1970); Leslie Thomas: *Come to the War* (Pan, 1969); and Nick Carter: *Assignment—Israel* (Tandem, 1967). Interested addicts can distinguish other Israel-based potboilers by the fact that the woman portrayed on the cover is usually partially clothed in khaki.

10. Philip Roth: *Portnoy's Complaint* (Random House, 1969).

11. Moshe Dayan: *Story of My Life* (Weidenfeld and Nicholson, 1976).

12. Hadassah Mor: *Burning Roads* (in Hebrew) (Kotz, 1963).

13. Michael Elkins: "Dayan's Story," in *The Jerusalem Post,* September 3, 1976.

14. Yael Dayan: *New Face in the Mirror* (Signet, 1960), and *Envy the Frightened* (Weidenfeld and Nicholson, 1961).

15. Yael Dayan: *Yael Dayan Israel Journal: June 1967* (McGraw-Hill, 1967).

16. Dahn Ben-Amotz: "Parents' Day," in *The New Israeli Writers,* ed. Dalia Rabikovitz (Sabra Books, 1969).

17. Bruno Bettelheim: *The Children of the Dream* (Macmillan, 1967).

18. Quoted by Amos Elon, *op. cit.*

19. The English version is called *The Seventh Day: soldiers talk about the Sixth Day War,* ed. Avraham Shapira (English version edited by Henry Near) (Penguin, 1970).

20. Amos Elon, *op. cit.*

21. Kalman Benyamini, in a paper presented at the Conference on Research on Israeli Youth sponsored by the Eshkol Institute of the Hebrew University of Jerusalem, May 1976.

22. In David Schoenbrun: *The New Israelis* (Atheneum, 1973).

23. From Yehuda Amichai: "Hike with a Woman," in *Yehuda Amichai: Selected Poems* (Penguin, 1971), translated by Harold Schimmel.

24. Malka Maon: *Socialization for Fulfilling Sex Roles in Israel's State School System* (in Hebrew) M.A. thesis in psychology at the Hebrew University of Jerusalem, 1974. Shulamit Kaufman found a similar pattern in kindergarten books in her M.A. thesis in education at Tel Aviv University: *Sexual Stereotypes and Sex Roles in Israeli Primers* (in Hebrew).

25. Kalman Benyamini, in a paper presented at the Convention of the Israel Psychological Association, Haifa, October 1975.

26. Eleanor Maccoby: "Sex Differences in Intellectual Functioning," in *The Development of Sex Differences*, ed. E. Maccoby (Stanford University Press, 1966).

27. Dalia Rabikovitz: "Clockwork Doll," in *Fourteen Israeli Poets: a selection of modern Hebrew poetry*, ed. Dennis Silk (Andre Deutsch, 1976). Translated by Dom Moraes.

CHAPTER 5. SEX AND SECURITY

1. From Robert Graves and Raphael Patai: *Hebrew Myths, the book of Genesis* (McGraw-Hill, 1966).

2. For instance, in the *Alpha Beta di Ben Sira*, in the Babylonian Talmud, and in the cabbalistic *Zohar*.

3. Lilly Rivlin: "Lilith," in *Ms.*, December 1972.

4. Robert Graves and Raphael Patai, *op. cit.*

5. *Ibid.*

6. Joseph Caro: *Shulhan Aruch.* The English version, an abridged one, is the *Code of Jewish Law*, ed. Rabbi Solomon Ganzfried (Hebrew Publishing Company, 1927).

7. Bronislaw Malinowski describes how the Melanesians coined this term in *The Sexual Life of Savages* (Routledge and Kegan Paul, 1929).

8. Article on Joseph Caro in the *Encyclopedia Judaica* (Keter, 1971).

9. In *Women on the Kibbutz* (in Hebrew) (Kibbutz HaMeuchad, 1959), an anthology of anecdotes, poems and speeches by and about women in the early days of the kibbutz.

10. Yonina Talmon: *Family and Community in the Kibbutz* (Harvard University Press, 1972).

11. Amos Elon: *The Israelis: Founders and Sons* (Holt, Rinehart and Winston, 1971).

12. Yonina Talmon, *op. cit.*

13. Meyer Levin: *The Settlers* (W. H. Allen, 1972).

14. In *Women on the Kibbutz, op. cit.*

15. Yitzhak Orpaz: *City of No Refuge* (in Hebrew) (Kibbutz HaMeuchad, 1972).

16. See Marc Feigin Fasteau: *The Male Machine* (McGraw-Hill, 1974).

17. Moshe Lancet *et al.: Sexual Behavior, Attitudes and Knowledge of Adolescents* (in Hebrew) (Israel Institute of Applied Social Research, for the Demographic Center, 1974), and Moshe Lancet *et al: Sexual knowledge and behavior of Israeli adolescents,* a paper presented at the Second International Symposium on Sex Education, Tel Aviv, June 1974.

18. Helen Antonovsky *et al.: Sexual attitude/behavior discrepancy among Israeli adolescent girls* (Demographic Center, Prime Minister's Office, Jerusalem, 1976).

19. "Safe estimates" from investigative journalist Baruch Nadel, who is writing a book on prostitution in Israel.

20. For instance, see Yehuda Rimmerman: "The Delinquent Girl—Her Problems and Distress," in *Saad,* March 1976; and Amiram Calfon: "Girls on the Way Down," in *Saad,* March 1975 (both in Hebrew).

21. Rivka Bar-Yosef *et al.: Women's Attitudes to Family Life* (in Hebrew) (Hebrew University of Jerusalem, 1973).

22. Rivka Bar-Yosef and Beverly Mizrachi: *Students' Attitudes to Family Life* (in Hebrew) (Hebrew University of Jerusalem, 1971).

23. "The Girls of Israel," in *Playboy,* April 1970.

24. Tamar Meroz: "The Unliberated Woman" and "Sex and the Stars" (in Hebrew), in *Ha'aretz,* March 9, 1973.

25. Andrew Meisels: *Six Other Days* (Pyramid, 1973).

26. Yael Dayan: *Dust* (Weidenfeld and Nicholson, 1963).

27. Rollo May: *Love and Will* (Norton, 1969).

CHAPTER 6. THE SWORD AND THE PLOWSHARE

1. During her visit to Israel in June 1973, Betty Friedan experienced a turnabout from admiration of sexual equality on the kibbutz to disillusionment on firsthand observation. Simone de Beauvoir's estimation that Israeli women are "very close to" equality was based largely on her impressions of kibbutz life, published in *New Outlook*, May 1967.

2. *U.S. News and World Report*, June 28, 1976.

3. All quotes from Chen Commanding Officer Dalia Raz are from my interview with her on June 18, 1976.

4. At a seminar on women in the army, organized by the Israel Association of University Women, Tel Aviv, December 25, 1975.

5. Tamar Breznitz-Svidovsky: *Israeli Women on the Home Front: reactions to pressure and coping mechanisms*, a paper presented at the First International Conference on Psychological Stress and Adjustment in War and Peace, Tel Aviv, January 1975.

6. From *Chen—The Women's Corps*, a pamphlet issued by the Israel Defense Forces.

7. Seminar on women in the army, *op. cit.*

8. In Yitzhak Abramovitz: "The Strong Side of the Weaker Sex" (in Hebrew), in *Maariv Lenoar*, April 22, 1975.

9. Edward Luttwak and Dan Horowitz: *The Israeli Army* (Allen Lane, 1975).

10. In the article "Because I don't complain" (in Hebrew), in *Al Hamishmar (Hotem)*, January 10, 1975.

11. Gideon Lev: "Company Clerks" (in Hebrew), in *Maariv*, January 8, 1975.

12. Ada Saar: column (in Hebrew) in *Al Hamishmar (Hotem)*, January 10, 1975.

13. Zeev Schiff: *A History of the Israel Army* (Straight Arrow, 1974).

14. Amos Perlmutter: *Military and Politics in Israel* (F. Cass, 1969).

15. Techiya Bat-Oren: *Women's Liberation—Whence?* (in Hebrew) (Boostan, 1975).

16. Except where otherwise stated, statistics are from Lionel Tiger and Joseph Shepher: *Women in the Kibbutz* (Harcourt Brace Jovanovich, 1976). While the demographic analyses in their book are excellent and more inclusive than previous ones, the conclusions

and interpretations are appallingly deterministic. The authors had the uncommon decency, however, to keep their statistical research and their commentary largely in separate sections of the book.

17. Yonina Talmon: *Family and Community in the Kibbutz* (Harvard University Press, 1972).

18. In *The Woman in the Kibbutz* (in Hebrew) (Givat Haviva, Kibbutz Research Center, July 21, 1974), selections from a seminar run by the Institute for Kibbutz Social Research at Givat Haviva, edited by Menahem Rosner, who heads the Institute and has written three excellent surveys on kibbutz women in the Artzi movement: "Women in the Kibbutz: Changing Status and Concepts," in *Asian and African Studies*, 3, 1967; "Changes in the Concept of Women's Equality in the Kibbutz" (in Hebrew), in *The Kibbutz Interdisciplinary Research Review*, 1973; and (together with Michal Palgi) "Sexual Equality in the Kibbutz—Regression or Qualitative Change?" (in Hebrew) (Givat Haviva, 1976).

19. In *Hashavua*, May 28, 1976 (in Hebrew), an issue devoted entirely to problems of women on the kibbutz.

20. Menahem Rosner: *Conclusions on Research on Women in the Kibbutz* (in Hebrew) (Givat Haviva, 1966).

21. Menahem Rosner and Michal Palgi: *Survey of Women Moving into Production and Central Administrative Tasks During and After the Yom Kippur War* (in Hebrew) (Givat Haviva, May 1974).

22. Lionel Tiger and Joseph Shepher, *op. cit.*

23. In Yaacov Friedler: "Ploughshares to Nurseries," in *The Jerusalem Post*, June 25, 1976.

24. In *Hashavua* (in Hebrew), May 1966.

25. A. I. Rabin: "Some Sex Differences in the Attitudes of Kibbutz Adolescents," in *Israel Annals of Psychiatry*, 1968.

26. Dar, Y.: *Sex Differences in Academic Achievements Among Kibbutz High-School Students* (in Hebrew) (Ichud Research Institute, Tel Aviv, 1974).

27. Lionel Tiger and Joseph Shepher, *op. cit.*

28. In Ada Maimon: *Women Build a Land* (Herzl Press, 1962).

CHAPTER 7. MARRIAGE—THE NATIONAL
PANACEA

1. From Diana Lerner: "The Wedding Extravaganza—a fact of Israeli life today," in *The Jerusalem Post*, October 22, 1976.

2. In Nikki Stiller: "Peace without Honor—the Battle of the Sexes in Israel," in *Midstream,* May 1976.

3. In *Time,* April 12, 1976, cover story on Rhodesia.

4. Statistics from the *U.N. Demographic Yearbook.*

5. Esther Goshen-Gottstein: *Marriage and First Pregnancy: cultural influences on attitudes of Israeli women* (Tavistock, 1966).

6. Rivka Bar-Yosef et al.: *Women's Attitudes to Family Life* (in Hebrew) (Hebrew University of Jerusalem, 1973).

7. Amos Oz: *My Michael* (Bantam, 1976).

8. In V. D. Segre's *Israel: A Society in Transition* (Oxford University Press, 1971), a book which is, for the most part, a good introduction to Israeli society.

9. Rivka Bar-Yosef and Zvia Levy: *Perception of Women's Roles on the Part of Seventeen-Year-Old Girls* (in Hebrew) (Work and Welfare Research Institute, Hebrew University of Jerusalem, 1976).

10. Rivka Bar-Yosef et al.: *Women's Attitudes to Family Life,* op. cit.

11. Zeev Schiff: *A History of the Israel Army* (Straight Arrow, 1974).

12. Rivka Bar-Yosef et al.: *Women's Attitudes to Family Life,* op. cit.

13. Phyllis Palgi: "The Adaptability and Vulnerability of Family Types in the Changing Israeli Society," in *Children and Families in Israel,* ed. Arieh Jarus et al. (Gordon and Breach, 1970).

14. Lea Shamgar-Hendelman: *War Widows in Israeli Society,* doctoral thesis for Sociology Department, Hebrew University of Jerusalem, 1977 (in Hebrew).

15. Golda Meir: *My Life* (Steimatzky, 1975).

CHAPTER 8. THE POLITICAL CHALLENGE

1. Yigael Yadin at press conference announcing the formation of his Democratic Movement party, Jerusalem, November 22, 1976.

2. Shaul Fogel at meeting of *Shalom Achshav* on women's liberation, Jerusalem, September 28, 1976.

3. Tamar Eshel: " '*Naamat*' and Women's Liberation" (in Hebrew), in *Maariv,* October 13, 1976.

4. Survey by the Israel Institute for Applied Social Research, for Member of Knesset Shulamit Aloni, August 1975.

5. In Helga Dudman: "Retreat on the Feminist Front," in *The Jerusalem Post*, February 12, 1976.

6. Prime Minister Yitzhak Rabin: "Greetings on the Occasion of International Women's Year," a speech to the Knesset on February 12, 1975 (Government Press Office Bulletin).

7. *Interim Report of the Prime Minister's Commission on the Status of Women* (in Hebrew), December 1976.

8. *The Third Hour—Divorce,* screened on Israel Television, November 13, 1976.

9. Tamar Breznitz-Svidovsky: *Israeli Women on the Home Front: reactions to pressure and coping mechanisms,* a paper presented at the First International Conference on Psychological Stress and Adjustment in War and Peace, Tel Aviv, January 1975.

10. Nola Chilton interviewed by Moshe Natan in "Women in War," in *Maariv,* January 18, 1974.

11. Joseph Campbell: *Myths to Live By* (Viking, 1972).

Index

About the Author

Lesley Hazleton received her B.A. from Manchester University, England, and her M.A. in Psychology from Hebrew University of Jerusalem. A resident of Jerusalem and a British and Israeli citizen, she has been an editor, a reporter for *The Jerusalem Post,* and a teacher. From 1973 to the present she has been a stringer for Time–Life's Jerusalem bureau.